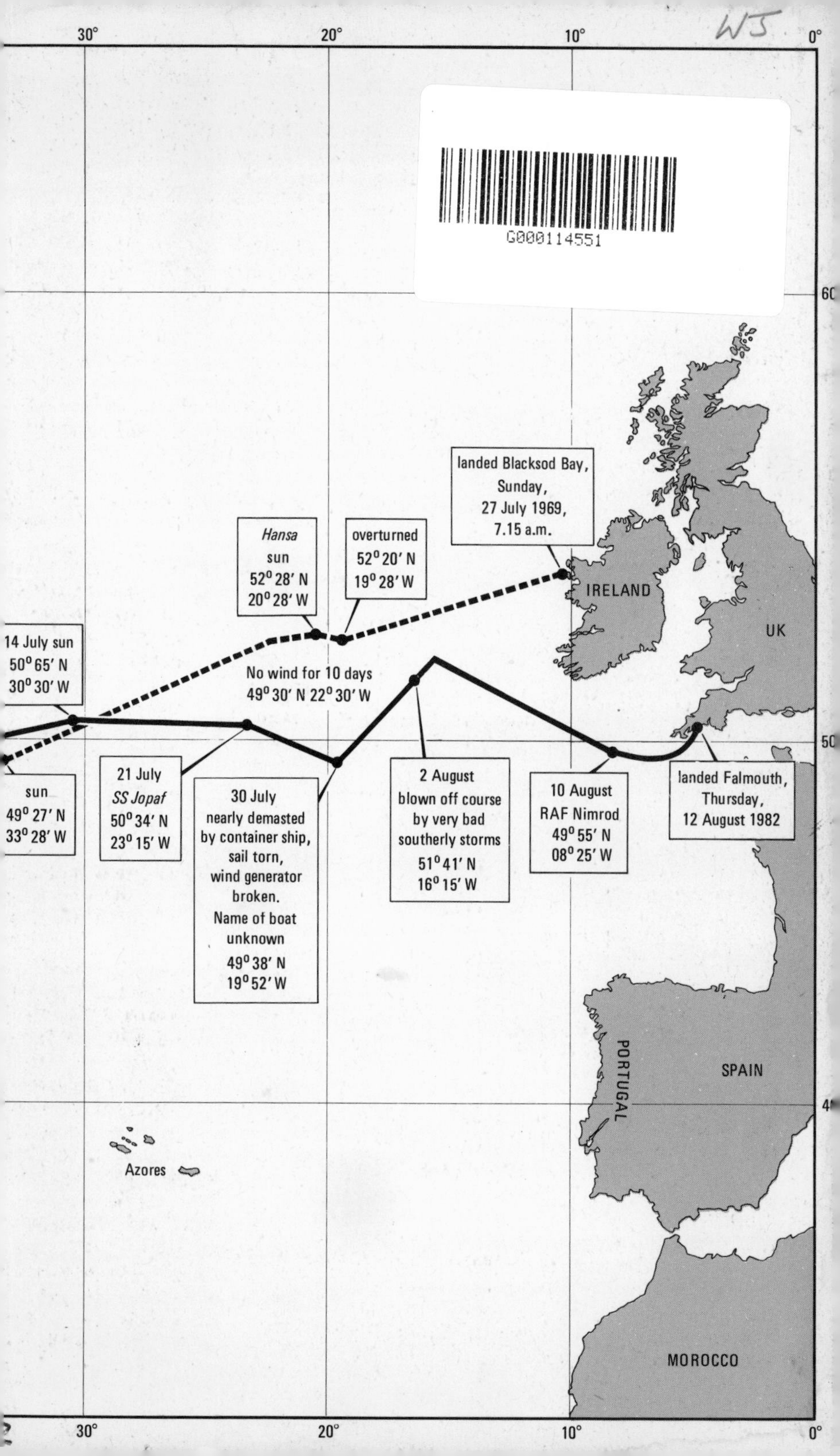

WJ
G000114551
30°
20°
10°
0°
60
50
40
landed Blacksod Bay,
Sunday,
27 July 1969,
7.15 a.m.
Hansa
sun
52° 28′ N
20° 28′ W
overturned
52° 20′ N
19° 28′ W
IRELAND
UK
14 July sun
50° 65′ N
30° 30′ W
No wind for 10 days
49° 30′ N 22° 30′ W
sun
49° 27′ N
33° 28′ W
21 July
SS Jopaf
50° 34′ N
23° 15′ W
30 July
nearly demasted
by container ship,
sail torn,
wind generator
broken.
Name of boat
unknown
49° 38′ N
19° 52′ W
2 August
blown off course
by very bad
southerly storms
51° 41′ N
16° 15′ W
10 August
RAF Nimrod
49° 55′ N
08° 25′ W
landed Falmouth,
Thursday,
12 August 1982
PORTUGAL
SPAIN
Azores
MOROCCO

Rough Passage

A Life of Adventure

Tom McClean with
Alec Beilby

Hutchinson/Stanley Paul
London Melbourne Sydney Auckland Johannesburg

Hutchinson/Stanley Paul & Co. Ltd

An imprint of the Hutchinson Publishing Group

17–21 Conway Street, London W1P 6JD

Hutchinson Group (Australia) Pty Ltd
30–32 Cremorne Street, Richmond South, Victoria 3121
PO Box 151, Broadway, New South Wales 2007

Hutchinson Group (NZ) Ltd
32–34 View Road, PO Box 40–086, Glenfield, Auckland 10

Hutchinson Group (SA) Pty Ltd
PO Box 337, Bergvlei 2012, South Africa

First published 1983
© Tom McClean 1983

MAC
892556

Set in Linotron Palatino by
Rowland Phototypesetting Ltd
Bury St Edmunds, Suffolk

Printed in Great Britain by The Anchor Press Ltd
and bound by Wm Brendon & Son Ltd,
both of Tiptree, Essex

ISBN 0 09 152530 6

I should like to dedicate this book to
Jill, James and Ryan.
Also to all those who helped
make the passage a little less rough
than it might have been

Contents

Photographic Acknowledgements

The publisher would like to thank the following for permission to use copyright photographs:

Express Newspapers (Super Silver; leaving the kipper factory workshop; launching at Mallaig; Transatlantic II); Dick Green (anxious moments of farewell; raring to go); Ambrose Greenway (home on the range; Jessie and Donald Macdonald; Loch Nevis; Tom and family); Popperfoto (Sir Ernest Shackleton). Other photographs were provided by the author

Preface

Some people may think that to write one's own life story when only forty years old is the last word in conceit, but the decision to do so was made for me. At the 1983 London International Boat Show I shared a special stand with my American friend and rival Bill Dunlop. His little boat *Wind's Will* lay next to *Giltspur* under a banner proclaiming us to be the 'Atlantic Sailors'. Considerable publicity was given to our presence at Earl's Court where, for ten days, Bill and I, helped by our wives, came face to face with the public.

As well as the hundreds of strangers who came and talked to us were many old friends who, having heard that I was there, called to see me. My address book on the stand, reserved for those old friends and some new ones that I made at the Boat Show, was almost filled. One moment that particularly pleased me, patriot that I am, was when Police Sergeant Peter Nelson, visiting the show with his wife and two children, signed the book 'Nelson of Trafalgar'. As the most direct descendant of Admiral Lord Nelson, he works in his spare time helping to build a large sailing ship to be crewed by able-bodied and disabled people. The ship will be called *Lord Nelson*.

After talking to him and many others, I realized just how interested people were in what I had done, what I am doing and why I have done it all. I wrote a book after my transatlantic rowing trip, but that was primarily about the voyage and that period of my life. People, many people, friends and strangers alike, wanted to know more.

Several publishers had already sown the seeds of the idea, suggested various titles for a book and offered contracts. After the Boat Show, with my plans to regain Dunlop's record for the Atlantic crossing in the smallest boat, I headed home to my base at Ardintigh. While the stormy winter winds howled around my little house I began to tell the whole story, trying to tell it as it was and trying not to leave out the many people who made all the things I have done possible. Some may have been forgotten. To them my apologies.

Obviously, in a life where one has met challenges head on, there have been moments and places where, for one reason or another, it is perhaps best to leave names out of the story. I have done this where feelings might be hurt, where it may be politically expedient not to mention those names, or in a few cases, where I have simply forgotten them or never knew them.

Finally, I would like to thank those who helped me pull the book together: Jill, my wife, who encouraged me even though there were plenty of things that needed to be done around our home; and Alec Beilby, of the *Sunday Express*, who met me when I reached Falmouth after my transatlantic sailing voyage and then helped me write my story for the *Express*. Much midnight oil was burned amid the arrival celebrations at that time. I should also like to thank him for helping with this book, showing me how to put things in the right order, editing where necessary, occasionally bullying me to get on with it, and for checking the proofs.

Tom McClean
Ardintigh
Scotland
March 1983

1 Early Days

The big steam engine wheezed, the carriages creaked and groaned as they weaved their way across the tangle of points outside Euston Station. The Irish boat train had reached London. It was a wet autumn day in 1947, although I only know this from what others have told me. Once the train had stopped a kindly lady approached the guard's van from which the guard passed one small boy and one tatty suitcase.

'This is number 28, McClean. Yours, I think,' he said, handing me out to her.

She took me, placed me on the platform and we walked to a car parked nearby. I had arrived, aged three and a half years, at the start of what was to be almost twelve years of constant battle for survival.

We were driven to Yardley Gobion, a small village near Stony Stratford, where Fegans Orphanage owned a large house. I can still remember that house, grey and daunting. They say that an early shock or change stimulates the memory, for whereas some people can go no farther back than about their fourth birthday, I can recall my arrival at Fegans with some clarity.

Indirectly, the journey to Fegans had begun over three years earlier. Until recently, I believed that my parents had been killed in a fire soon after I was born in Dublin in 1943. I knew that as a baby I had been fostered out to a family in County Wicklow to the south of Dublin. A lady, whom I called Auntie Kay, supervised the fostering.

It was while checking a few facts in order to write this book that I uncovered the truth. There was no fire. It was a kindly tale thought up by those involved in my early life to stop me wondering about my Mum and Dad. What actually happened was different. After I was born, my mother, whose sight was failing, could not cope with me. She and my father, meanwhile, were not getting along very well, so I was taken from them and sent to the Wicklow family. By the time I was three it was apparent that my foster parents, who had other children, were finding it hard to look after me, so Auntie Kay decided that, with life in Ireland being as hard as it was, I might have a better start if I were sent to England. So it was onto the mail boat at Dun Laoghaire, with a label numbered 28 tied to me and my case, and off to England, passed like a parcel from person to person as the long journey progressed.

Fegans Orphanage at Yardley Gobion looked after boys from birth to the age of eleven at which age they were moved to the main orphanage in the centre of Stony Stratford. The junior home was a tough but kindly place and when I arrived I was the youngest and smallest boy there. The home was run by women, with a Miss Hayes and Sister Mary in charge. They weren't nuns, but they dressed as if they were, and the religious training was rigorous. We had Bible classes every day, twice on Sundays.

There was nothing like family life as I understand it today. The staff were kind but very strict. Obviously they thought they were doing a good job, and they were, but at the time we did not appreciate it. It was a matter of 'them and us' as we marched around in our grey shorts, flannelette shirts and lace-up black boots. Food was poor and we fought among ourselves to get enough to eat. I learned to fight early on and was often beaten for it, but it was to stand me in good stead when I moved on to the big school, as we called Fegans in Stony Stratford.

I was a stubborn boy right from the start, and was often punished. Punishment for breaking Yardley's multitude of rules ranged from long periods of standing on a painted line looking straight ahead to a beating with a belt. I must have been fairly tough, because when being beaten you were quite rightly expected to cry, but I used to laugh. This made the staff hit me even harder, and the harder they wielded the belt the more I would hop about laughing.

From our earliest days at Yardley we looked forward to going to the big boys' school. We started lessons at the age of five, the classes being held in the house, but when we were seven we went to the local school, out each morning, back each evening.

There was some land adjoining the house where we were allowed to play. One of my greatest joys at that time was to build houses out of turves. We would stack the turf, one piece on top of the next, and put a roof over the top. It was my first try at building and I was to do plenty more during the years ahead.

We did not make close friends. There were boys whom one liked a little more than others, but I made no real pal in those early hard days. Friends came later.

I did make one special friend at Yardley, however: Mr Gardener, who was the gardener there. I used to enjoy walking with him among the vegetables, learning which was which and how they were grown. He was a Scot, originally from Arbroath, and he taught me a great deal. I liked him and when I eventually left the orphanage I went back to see him when I was in the area. I also used to call and see Miss Hayes during these visits. I suppose the fact that I did go back means that, though tough, life had had its moments of happiness.

Finally, in 1953, the great day came to move to the big school in Stony Stratford. Apart from my school clothes and washing kit I owned nothing, so packing for the move did not take long. I was put in Livingstone House, the smallest and the youngest of about thirty boys. I could tell as soon as I arrived that it was not going to be the heaven that I had imagined.

Perhaps, to give some idea of life there, it would be best to describe a typical day during school term time, a day that was virtually the same for almost five years. Before seven each morning the masters would hammer on the dormitory door and we would leap out of bed, kneel on the floor for five minutes and pretend to pray. Then, gathering our coarse towels from the end of the beds, we would run down the spiral staircase, across the quadrangle to the cold washrooms and have a strip wash. Then we were inspected in front of large lamps, a master known by us as the Jailer, ticking our names off against our number. My number was now 82, and 82 was to top the punishment list on many occasions.

We would then run back to the dormitory, make our beds, folding blankets and sheets in a bed block army style, and dress, putting on our working clothes. Off again across the quadrangle to the assembly hall, having been inspected again and ticked off on one of the lists. In the assembly hall we would wait for the duty bell boy who would ring a vast brass bell. We would rush off to the dining rooms, one dining room to each of the four houses into which we were divided. Food was basic: breakfast a simple meal of porridge, tea and bread thinly spread with margarine, sometimes an egg floating in a sea of grease or, on very rare occasions, bacon or a sausage. Eating, like everything else, was competitive. If you put your knife down on your plate, another boy would shout 'Overboard' and grab your food. The only way to survive was not to stop eating from the moment the food arrived. The meal, of course, began with grace. How much food you were given depended upon how well you got on with the bigger boy serving it. Throughout the meal the masters walked around the tables trying to keep order by striking the tables and boys with canes.

After breakfast we went back to the dormitory to sweep and tidy the rooms. We then put on our best uniform, ready to be marched out into the town to the local school. Again we were inspected and ticked off on a list before going to the quadrangle to wait for the gates into the High Street to be opened.

Can you imagine it, fifty boys, some as old as fifteen, in boots, shorts, grey shirts and jackets, marching along the street holding hands! Holding hands – it was certain to raise catcalls from the town kids, and did, but our time was to come.

The bell rang again, the gates opened and we were off in crocodile. Once inside the local school, all fifty of us used to line up. The town kids were there and we, in turn, lined them up. Pocket money, sweets, anything they had was taken. If they had not brought anything then we gave them a thumping and told them to bring something the next day or they would be thumped again. That was how we dealt with the boys, many of whom had jeered at us on our way to school. The girls were different. We used to tie them up in the lavatories and tease them, but never actually harmed them.

I found most of the classes boring. I enjoyed history and geography but much of what we were taught was uninteresting and taught by people who did not seem to care whether we learned or not. Still, it passed the time and was a change from Fegans. Though I disliked the academic subjects, I did enjoy the practical things such as wood and metal working. I made a wooden stool and on one occasion when I went back to Ireland for a holiday I gave it to Auntie Kay. It still has pride of place in her house.

School over, we were marched back to the orphanage. By now we had passed the money that we had taken from the other kids to one chosen Fegans boy. The sweets and other goodies were shared out among us. As we marched back we would wait until the master in charge had been distracted and then, at the right moment, the chosen boy would make a break for it, dashing into a food or sweet shop to buy what we needed. He made his way back into Fegans by cutting round the orphanage and coming in through the playing field. We then divided the spoils.

Although I didn't find the school very exciting, I liked Mr Read, the headmaster, a tall gaunt man, strict but fair. Later, during one of my visits to Stony Stratford I included him in my list of people to see. He, in turn, wrote to me following one of my later adventures in the Atlantic.

Back at the orphanage we were locked in and sent up to the dormitory to change into our working clothes, wash and brush-up and be checked against yet another list, following an inspection before tea. This was again a battle for food where chaos prevailed and good manners were ignored in the interests of survival. After tea, the last main meal of the day, we were free for about an hour unless we had a red star against our names. This meant we had to carry out correction duties. Red stars were earned for swearing, fighting, untidiness or any of a hundred crimes that were out of order at Fegans. Punishments ranged from a beating with a cane, often six or more strokes, to extra manual work. The manual work could be anything from digging up plantains, weeds, on the playing field to scrubbing the quadrangle with a very small brush on our hands and knees. Almost all punishment work involved keeping the place clean. I became an expert at cleaning floors, walls and windows.

After the evening recreation hour we assembled in the main hall again for prayers and a reading from the Bible. More inspections, washing and being checked off on lists before going up to the dormitory to undress for bed. We were allowed about half an hour sitting in our beds reading or talking to one another before the masters came round to put the lights out. We would watch them as they crossed the quadrangle to their own quarters. Then all hell broke loose. Pillow fights, fist fights for sweets or, for those who smoked, for a few dogends of cigarettes picked up in the road on the way to and from school. Eventually the fighting, talking and ragging stopped and we went to sleep.

I used to fight for money. We used to be given 3d per week. One penny was banked for us, one put into the church collection each Sunday, and the third we could spend on sweets in the school tuck shop which was open on Friday evenings. The bigger boys would encourage the smaller boys who could fight to keep fit. I trained by doing press-ups, exercises and by heaving bricks about. I might have been small, but when paired off against boys from other houses I was unbeatable. The fights were a far shout from the Marquess of Queensberry's idea of boxing. Anything went, and usually did. I frequently won, earning some money for my sponsor and for myself. Sometimes the masters would organize fights themselves but more often they were busy trying to stop them.

Sundays were different from the rest of the week. We went to church three times that day, in the morning to the normal morning service, in the afternoon to Bible class, and again in the evening. The collection of our one penny would take place at the afternoon Bible reading and study class. I often wondered whether we got the same penny back the following week. The inspections were relentless as ever; up to thirty times a day in all we were ticked off on some list or other and more if under punishment.

The routine was much the same when the school closed for the holidays. The checks continued, getting-up time was as early as ever and lessons were replaced by long walks in the surrounding countryside, occasional visits to homes outside the orphanage and more time for games, which meant fighting. In the summer we would go as an entire group to a camp near Poole, living in tents on a heath near Poole Harbour. It was a riot. How the masters survived always remained a mystery, but we lived like wild men, and didn't seem to be too popular with the natives.

I went back to Ireland three or four times during my twelve years at the orphanage to see my Auntie Kay. Although she is not a real aunt, she is the closest person I have ever known, as close as any relative. She wrote to me throughout the time I was at Fegans and is still a very dear friend. Not family, but the next best sort of person and even better than many, from what I have since heard.

Apart from such breaks we never really saw the outside world. We were constantly warned and almost protected from that world, reputedly wicked and full of sin and crime. It sounded great; all we wanted to do was go out and try it. Certainly, without realizing it at the time, we were being given the training needed to face what lay ahead. The time was approaching for me to leave and my excitement was mixed with some apprehension. I was due to leave just after my fifteenth birthday.

The orphanage owned a farm in Sussex but the masters realized that although I liked growing things I was at my best as a carpenter. They arranged lodgings for me in Uckfield and signed me on as an apprentice carpenter. (About this time the farm, where a religious atmosphere was maintained, closed down through lack of money, or profits.) I was given a carpenter's tool kit worth about £50, a great deal of money in those days, 1958, when a good wage was £10 a week. I enjoyed the work, went out in the evenings and still had a few shillings left at the end of it. Life was good, but I had taken to the Teddy Boy cult, drainpipe trousers, wide-lapelled jacket with razor blades tucked under the collar, and thick-soled shoes.

My digs were fine. Mr Brett was a retired butcher and Mrs Brett was a homely sort of person who seemed to understand that I needed to stretch my wings a little. They never worried me or worried about me. It was a whole new world for me and I enjoyed it, but the carpentry in the firm at the end of the road in which the Bretts lived seemed a bit quiet – and £50 easy money was staring me in the face. I left the job, sold the tool kit, pocketed the money and signed on with the Buxted Chicken Company. It was a different world as far as I was concerned, not the job but the people who worked there, about fifty in all including at least thirty young girls.

My new job was easy. It involved cutting the feet off 11,000 dead chickens a day as they came past on a conveyor belt. Nowadays, as I look back, it seems the sort of thing to drive me mad, but the company, the fun, the chat and the constant music passed the time, while the evenings were spent in pubs drinking Stingo or Merrydown cider. Under age though I was, I never seemed to have trouble in getting served in pubs and began to reckon that I was a bit of a lad with the girls.

The news of my defection from the wood-working company to the wicked atmosphere of the chicken factory was not well received at Fegans; even less so the fact that I had disposed of my tool kit and spent the money. I was removed from Sussex and sent to Hartwell Hill Farm, near Aylesbury in Buckinghamshire, run by John Venn. John and Pauline Venn ran a 300-acre mixed farm. They had three children, Cliff, Greg and Hilary, and I was treated as one of the family. I still am. Along with my Auntie Kay's home in Ireland, Hartwell Hill Farm is one of two places that I have always regarded, since I first went there, as home.

The farm had a herd of about seventy Friesian milking cows as well as more than a hundred beef cattle and a hundred acres put down to barley and wheat. I liked the work, hard though it was and different from the life in Sussex. Up at dawn to clean out calf stalls, hump milk, many different physical jobs. It toughened me up and filled me out. I had never done any hard physical work until then and was small in stature. Farming was good for me, that was certain. We would go to the cattle market and I took one day off every fortnight; it was all I needed. The Venns taught me to save money, providing me with a bank book. I was beginning to grow up and understand more about the civilized way to live, but after about ten months I began to get itchy feet.

I used to phone one of my friends, Sam McCarthy, also an ex-Fegans boy, who lived in Sussex. Because of the defunct farm to which many of us had been sent before it closed down, there were many Fegans boys in Sussex and we kept in touch. Another was Bernard Waltham, whom we called Snowy. He was one of about 20 per cent of Fegans boys who did not make it and settle down in the outside world. He dropped out, became a bit of a hippy and a few years ago I heard that he had been found dead in a ditch. He was the exception rather than the rule, I am pleased to say. Many went off to do their National Service and stayed on in the forces, while others are today successful in business. Fegans had taught us survival and that, after all, is what the big world is all about.

Sam told me that he could find me some digs and a job so, for the first time in my life, apart from the thwarted excursion to the chicken factory, I set off to make my own way.

I went back to my original lodgings with the Bretts and began work on a building site as a hod carrier, taking loads of bricks up scaffolding to the bricklayers. My quota was a thousand bricks a day for which, after a five-day week, I was paid £15, a good wage then. What was more, I could finish the job by lunch time and have the rest of the day off.

The first building job lasted about three months. Then I moved on, as I was to do through fifteen other jobs over the time between leaving the Venns and joining the army. I was never out of work, always improving my wages and always enjoying life. I was a fully fledged Teddy Boy by now, chasing the girls, going to Brighton prom to walk up and down with the other Teds and be part of the scene, both down there and in London. At that time Sam told me that he had been to Brighton and signed on in the Parachute Regiment, a tough mob, he told me. I was surprised, but the idea began to appeal to me too. As I was too young to sign on, I went on working the building sites.

I was a member of the Uckfield Youth Club, a great place to meet the girls, and used to take part in club activities, including one event, at weekends, in which we had to get as far from Uckfield as possible in a given time and phone in to say where we were. One of these schemes was held just before Sam set off for Aldershot, so I teamed up with him.

'Bugger that for a game,' he said, 'we'll go up to London and have a bit of a laugh.'

We stole a motorbike and set off for London. Every time we covered twenty miles or so we stopped, left the bikes and took two more.

We reached London and cruised around, both now on the same bike, Sam driving, as we went along the King's Road, Chelsea. Suddenly, right in front of us was a squad car ordering us to stop. We tried to make a dash for it but we both fell off the bike right in the middle of Sloane Square. There were coppers everywhere chasing us and after a run through several side streets we decided to go quietly, as they say – quietly, right to Bow Street police station and a night in cells before going to court next day. We thought it a great joke, no real harm having been done, but the magistrate, who seemed to spend most of his morning sentencing prostitutes and drunks, took a dim view and bound us over to keep the peace for a year, giving us a real ticking-off.

We went back to Sussex. Sam then left for the training depot in Aldershot and I for another stint on the buildings. Life was fun, but one really has to let off steam at that age and the scope for doing this in the fifties was limited. Hard work was not the cure; there was plenty of that in my life. Even the old Matchless motorbike which I had bought, and which I frequently fell off, answered none of those deep-down frustrations. Something had to blow. I needed some sort of a challenge. It was three months later, when Sam reappeared in Uckfield in his uniform with tales of the training, that I made up my mind. The Parachute Regiment sounded exactly what I wanted to do. I went to Brighton, took some tests, passed, and was told to come back in a couple of months when I was exactly seventeen and a half.

2 The High Jump: Into the Paras

I returned to Brighton on the appointed day in my best clothes, was given a rail warrant and headed off to Aldershot. From the moment our batch reached Aldershot station until three months later our feet never seemed to touch the ground. I loved it. Para Regiment training was like a kids' tea party after Fegans, although you could not make some of the others there believe that. We did forced road marches, cross-country runs, learned to shoot, fight, march and keep ourselves smart. As usual, I was the youngest and certainly the smallest in the platoon, so I had to make an extra effort to keep ahead of the rest. On a training run over a tank training area, rutted with tank tracks, I tried so hard that I was in a state of collapse at the finish, but I was well up in front with the leaders and our instructors seemed pleased.

To me the army seems, as I look back, to have been the turning point in my life. Now I believe that some of the kids who are on the dole, bored, lost, fed up with life, would really benefit from some sort of national service, not necessarily military service, but from doing something to benefit other people, helping the country, contributing to the general welfare. It would give them a sense of pride in where they live and what they are.

The early days in the army taught me something else, too. Books. Though I had learned to read, I had hardly read a single book before joining the army; magazines, comics, that sort of thing, sure, but a book? Never. There was a library at the Aldershot depot and we were encouraged to use it. There I discovered the works of Shackleton and Scott, and these books became a source of great happiness to me as well as setting a challenge and, later, an example.

The training for the Parachute Regiment was hard, mentally and physically, with the emphasis on the physical aspect. Two months, maybe more, of running, marching, assault courses and long forced marches with full equipment; it beat more than a few of those who started the training course, but I thrived on it. The whole business was designed to prepare us for the real task of the regiment, parachuting. As we approached the end of the basic course, emerging as infantrymen, we were taken to start ground training in readiness for our first jumps.

Parachute training was carried out at Abingdon where, in a big hangar, we learned how to fall, use the harness, pack chutes and carry out the emergency drills in case our main parachute, on our backs, did not open. Then the big day came, the first jump from a barrage balloon sent up on a wire from a trailer, the basket containing two nervous trainees and a jump master suspended underneath. Anyone who says that he is not nervous during those early jumps is a liar, but the long training had prepared us for the moment and when my turn came I dropped down through the trap in the floor of the basket quite pleased to be away from that swaying box. I was on the ground before I had had time to take it all in. My first jump, cheers. This was the life for me. The second jump, again from the basket, was a bigger strain on the nerves than the first, but after that it was down hill. We were off to do five more jumps from transport aircraft and each was more fun than the one before. Finally we made two jumps at night from aircraft and the great day came when we were presented with our red berets and Parachute Regiment brevets, wings, which we wore proudly.

I left the depot and was sent to join the 3rd Battalion of the regiment, 3 Para as we called it. I had passed out with good marks for most things – shooting, appearance, running, general physical fitness – but I hadn't, perhaps, done as well on the schooling side.

In the battalion I met someone who was, literally, to become my blood brother. Brendan Merrifield, an Irishman. We went out for evenings together and became great friends. Life for the next few months was a round of local exercises, parades, sport and training. I was a rifleman in 'C' Company.

Our first really big exercise was in Greece. Part of a NATO scheme called Exercise Fabulous, it turned out to be far from that for me. There was to be the biggest airborne drop since the war, the whole of 16 Independent Parachute Brigade, with the Greek Parachute Regiment acting as the enemy. Everything seemed to go well; the bosses on both sides appeared quite pleased with themselves.

After it was over we visited the Greek soldiers at their base. One of our people suggested that I ought to walk up the hill to see where the Greeks stored their weapons and ammunition. I liked, still like, weapons, so off I went. Their armoury was simply a big tent with rifles, light machine guns and the rest chained together, probably a thousand pieces of kit in total. The Greek paras' personal weapons were kept in a big chest in the corner of the tent. There were Sten guns, Colt 45s, the lot. I asked one of our people to show me the revolver he was holding. He turned round, pointed the gun at me as if to hand it over, when it went off, two feet away from me. As the bullet hit me I felt nothing. All I thought was, Bloody hell! What's happening? At that same moment another bloke let out a terrific scream and dashed from the tent holding his leg. He had been lying on a camp bed writing a letter.

The bullet had hit me in the lower part of my stomach, gone right through my bladder and pelvis, missing the bone, the veins, the nerves, the arteries, everything. It then blew off the left cheek of my buttocks, hit the other man in the leg, and buried itself in the ground. I stood there, swore at the man and collapsed. The man who had fired the gun was stunned. He dropped it and ran out of the tent.

I was bleeding like a stuck pig. Blood was pouring from me. I was told later that I would have lasted less than fifteen minutes if help had not been swift. Panic everywhere, people rushing about. The pain in my backside was terrible, as if the whole of my bum was on fire. Someone found a field dressing while someone else rolled me over onto my stomach and pulled my shorts down. They crammed an emergency field wound dressing into the vast wound to staunch the bleeding. Another chum gave me a piece of wood to bite on, which helped because when in intense pain one grinds one's teeth until they almost break.

While all this was happening another para had dashed off down the hill to get help and transport, a distance of about half a mile, maybe less. On the way he was met by the regimental sergeant major who was coming up the hill.

'Soldier, where's your beret?' the RSM screamed.

'Someone's been shot, badly wounded, sir. I'm off to get transport. He's probably dying,' replied the harassed soldier.

'I don't bloody care if World War Three has started, or the Queen's been shot. You don't go rushing around bloody Greece without your beret. Go and get it!'

The RSM, immaculate with pace stick under his arm, was not going to let a small matter like a rifleman being shot upset the standards. Back up the hill went the soldier, found his beret and ran down again to the motor transport depot, past the crimson-faced RSM.

All this time I thought I was dying, and as, at last, the Land Rover arrived I can just remember seeing it before finally passing out as I was loaded alongside the chap who had been hit in the leg. We were, I was later told, taken down the hill to the first-aid post and the medical officer. The first-aid post was a whitewashed building with two tents outside. A generator powered the lamps over the temporary operating table. Captain Hedges, an army doctor, who later went to the North Pole with the explorer Wally Herbert, was there, waiting for us. He did some tests for internal injuries and then decided to wait for a while before operating. I was given morphine and put on a drip, lapsing into a groggy coma, having recovered consciousness while Captain Hedges and his team, in Greece to mend paras who might have been bent during the jump, tested and probed.

Clamps were used to stop the bleeding and more dressings were applied. They then checked my blood group. B Negative, the same as most blue babies. Rare, and not carried in the supplies, so they had to put out a call for anyone with B Negative blood. They only found one in the whole battalion –

800 men – and that was my pal Brendan Merrifield. Normally for a blood transfusion they take one pint, but they took a full three pints from Brendan in one go. Three pints! That is about half of all there is in a fit man. After they had taken his blood, he was laid flat out in the bed next to mine.

After two hours of drips, blood, morphine and the rest, they started the operation. The hole in the front of my abdomen was small, but they had to cut a big slice from the bottom of my belly to above my navel to get at my bladder. They stitched the holes in my bladder and inserted two tubes, one to take liquid in and the other to take the fluid out to prevent blood clots. Then they turned me over and started on my backside where there was a huge hole. A lot of flesh and skin had been blown away. The wound was about 6 inches long, 2 or 3 inches wide and between 3 and 5 inches deep. I was told that they could very nearly see right through me.

They cleaned the wound down to good wholesome flesh and then packed the space with paraffin gauze dressings, leaving the top open so the wound could heal from the bottom. Two or three hours later the job was done as far as possible under field conditions. I came round a little later to see tubes and bottles draped around me and Brendan asleep alongside.

The next plan was to get me to a hospital. The drips and the bottle supplying my bladder were carried by an orderly as two stretcher bearers picked me up. We headed for the door of the first-aid post when the orderly dropped the bottles. As they smashed on the stone floor, all the pipes and other rigging were pulled out of the various holes. I passed out like a light. When I came to I was back on the operating table where they had opened everything up again, reinserted the pipes and tubes and sewn me up once more. They said that all was well, not to worry and they would soon have me on the way home.

The nearest military hospital, run by the British army, was in Malta. Two enormous coloured American GIs appeared and took me to a Medivac helicopter to fly me to the nearest airfield where a Hastings transport was already waiting. It was full of casualties from the drop – broken arms and legs, nothing too serious, but needing better treatment than could be provided by the field hospitals set up in Greece by the British army. I was strapped to my stretcher, arms tied by my side. I was airsick so a nurse brought a mask, tied it to my face and left me. I was sick again and choking with the vomit inside the mask. I could do nothing. I was drowning in vomit with the mask over my nose and mouth. I lay helpless, rolling my head from side to side. I wasn't even able to shout out for fear of choking further. At last a horrified nurse returned and I was saved. It was, for me, an awful flight, but we reached Malta where I was kept for five or six days until off the danger list.

The army had notified two people of the accident, my Auntie Kay and the Venns. Not really next of kin, but the best I could do. In Malta I quickly regained strength and was declared fit enough to be flown home by the RAF to Lyneham. From there I was taken to the Cambridge Military Hospital in Aldershot.

Once in the Cambridge, as it is known to all soldiers, I became known by the nursing staff as the Waterworks because of all the bottles and tubes that were still hanging out of and on various parts of me. The staff were wonderful, kind and understanding. It took ten weeks from the time of the shooting until I was able to leave hospital. The wound at the front healed well although I had a bladder infection; the wound on the other side, my bottom, gradually healed from the inside outwards, being clamped a little more each day. The final result was a scar on my stomach and a neat dimple on the left cheek of my backside. The worst part of the whole stay in hospital was when they removed the artificial exit from the bladder and told me to revert to my own equipment, unused for weeks. Passing red hot fusewire is the nearest comparison I can think of to describe the pain, but I persevered. In the end I was completely normal, ready to go back to jumping, marching and shooting. It had been a long ten weeks, but compensated for by all the help and care I experienced. I was now eighteen and had been in the army eight months.

Trouble had brewed up in the Middle East in 1962 and 3 Para was sent to Bahrain as a support force for the local troops.

There was no accommodation for us when we arrived so we lived in tents on the airfield while a work party was formed to build a permanent camp at the other end of the island – aluminium huts, made to reflect the heat of the Gulf sun. Silver City, we called it. Laying the concrete was hard, back-breaking work; the whole time we were on stand-by in case we had to go to Kuwait where trouble was threatening.

When the huts were built I managed to get an easy job in the supply store and it was while working here that I had long chats with the Battalion padre, Fred Preston, known to the soldiers as Fiery Fred. He wanted to buy a dhow and sail it back to Britain. He had found an old boat on a beach and had been granted funds from the regiment to renovate it in traditional style. He employed local craftsmen to do the carpentry work, using traditional drills, made like a bow and arrow, an adze, which is as old as the drill, and other ageless tools. To power the boat we managed to acquire an old three-cylinder Lister diesel engine, which I helped install.

Renovating the boat was good fun and relieved the monotony of waiting for something to happen, or not happen, at the northern end of the Persian Gulf. We worked for three or four months on the dhow until it was ready to sail. Fiery Fred said that we ought to give it a bit of a test run down the Persian Gulf to Dubai, 300 miles farther east.

On the day of departure Fred was away and we had a mixed crew of lame paras, some with sailing experience, some with none. One even had a broken leg. All in all five or six of us, a motley bunch. We had a wireless and carried weapons in case of pirates. Food consisted of army composite rations. We soon met a storm and a plank flew out of the hull letting water flood into the engine compartment which promptly filled with steam. Water was streaming in as we headed the boat into the wind and pumped for our lives, signalling a Mayday call for help. We were about a hundred miles from the coast and the storm showed little sign of lessening.

The RAF flew overhead and after about three hours, just as we were clearly losing the battle on the pumps, a patrol boat appeared. It was too rough for her to come alongside so we decided over the radio that she would make runs and we would leap across to her, one man at a time. When my turn came the patrol boat suddenly dropped away as I jumped, and I jumped so hard that I cleared the boat and landed in the sea. The crew managed to haul me aboard. The man with the broken leg made the leap with a cry of pain like a Japanese wrestler going into the attack, but he managed it.

Wet, cold and seasick, we were taken below and given pea soup laced with pepper. It was so thick you could stand your spoon upright in it. After that I felt better, really great, in fact. Then the patrol boat crew realized that there were weapons on board the dhow, now irretrievable, so they threw a note aboard her explaining who she belonged to, a curious thing to do. Sadly we left her. She eventually sank, the wreckage being driven ashore weeks later off the Emirate States coast. It was a sorry expedition, but we all survived despite the battalion's decision to crew the dhow with a boatload of cripples.

We were taken back to Bahrain by the patrol boat and met by our commanding officer whom we knew as Farrah the Para, Colonel Farrah-Hockley, who had already made a name for himself in the Gloster Regiment in Korea during the Battle of Imjin. One of his more extraordinary activities in the Paras was to organize the soldiers' wives into lines, like a parade, and then teach them to cook. He was more pleased with our expedition than we had dared to hope and awarded us a bottle of whisky each. Looking back now, I think he was simply pleased to see us back ashore in one piece. It had been my first encounter with the sea and although I had enjoyed it I was not sure whether I would ever make a sailor.

I was nineteen now and in the anti-tank platoon. I was very fit, running around with a 100-lb weight on my back. I had built a canoe before the business with the dhow while I had been working in the store. It was a simple boat, a frame covered with canvas, but I used to make expeditions along the coast of Bahrain, ten miles one way or ten miles the other.

Bahrain was not much of a place as far as I was concerned. It was a low-lying island, very smelly in those days, with the local Arabs seemingly spending most of their time praying, crapping in the sea or dodging around trying to steal our kit. They should have known better. I would go out and chat with the local road gangs, trying to get through to them in broken English and sharing their food – chappattis, flat dough-like spicy pancakes. It was all part of finding out how the other half of the world lived and helped fill in the long boring days we spent waiting in the Gulf for some action.

The action blew up in Aden and we were sent to give support to the troops already there, covering the British withdrawal from the town. What a place! Bahrain was a palace by comparison. It was back into tents again, at the airfield at Kormaksar, across the harbour from the town of Crater. That's exactly what it was, a bloody hole. At last, some action. We were to go into north Aden, into the Yemen where the SAS had been operating against the terrorists. One of the SAS patrols had been outnumbered by about twenty-five to one by the desert rebels. They had put up a fight and most managed to extricate themselves, but one SAS man had been captured. He was decapitated and his head displayed on a pole over the main gate of Sana. It was time to level the odds, so we were sent there to sort things out. We went right forward in company with Royal Marines to the Wadi Dipsan.

The enemy were rebel tribesmen, very able fighters who knew the land and, even with antiquated weapons, were good shots. In Aden we prepared for the move by doing fitness training, getting used to the sun and making long forced marches with heavy kit. We marched up to the area where we expected to meet the rebels and because, as an anti-tank platoon, we were without a job (the rebels had no tanks), we were made into a scouting platoon. We had no platoon commander as such, no officer, so we were led by the regimental sergeant major, Nobby Arnold, a great character, tough, hard and fair.

We moved slowly through the area, feeling very confident, when we suddenly came under fire from rifles at a range of about 1000 yards across the valley, the wadi. We all took cover. It was great fun, our first taste of being under fire for most of us. At nineteen it was a real adventure, a great game. We felt invincible. I was on the general purpose machine gun, the GPMG, a very good weapon. I was number one on the gun while Bloodbrother Brendan Merrifield was number two. It seemed as if the regiment wanted to keep the B

Negatives together, but whatever the reason, it suited us.

Nobby assessed the situation and spotted where the fire was coming from. Once he had done this and made a plan, we began moving towards the enemy, one section covering another as it went up, 'pepperpotting' we called it. We covered the rifle group by potting at the enemy. Then they would do the same for us as we moved up. Hard going, but exciting. There were twelve riflemen in a rifle section and just the two of us with the GPMG. The enemy were in some small buildings so, once we had gained the ridge above them, we kept giving them the odd shot to make them keep their heads down. The rifle group then broke up into twos and threes and pepperpotted right down to the bottom of the valley and up the other side. It was very hot, midday, and about 120° Fahrenheit. The operation took more than half an hour but no one moved from the buildings.

When the rifle section was near enough to the buildings to attack, Nobby raised his handkerchief as a signal to us and we held our fire while he and his men fixed bayonets. They charged, killing some of the opposition, wounding others and passing right through the position, forming up on the far side.

It was one of the very few bayonet charges carried out since the Second World War. Once they had regrouped on the far side of the huts and Brendan and I were about to start down the side of the valley to join them, I saw this cow moving slowly out from the huts towards our left flank. Nothing odd about that after all the shooting except that instead of four legs it had eight. It was 800 yards away across the valley. I fired a long burst, killing the cow and the two people hiding behind it who had been trying to escape.

Half an hour later, bathed in sweat, we joined the rifle group, our 100-lb packs feeling like lead weights. The prisoners consisted of four young men, two old men and a couple of women. Several dead lay outside the huts. We were allowed a smoke break, so we lined the prisoners up and put one man, McQuade, on guard over them while we made a brew of tea and some of the lads had a cigarette.

Suddenly one of the young prisoners grabbed the sentry by the throat, holding him really tightly. They were too close for us to shoot the attacker. McQuade's rifle dropped to the ground.

'Throw him down, McQuade,' we shouted and the tough McQuade threw the little Arab right over his head. The Arab, with a look of terror in his eyes, jumped up and ran like a rabbit along the side of the wadi.

'Let me have him!' shouted one of the lads. 'I'll get him!' yelled another, but it was a Jock called Hackston who took a superb rifle shot at 300 or 400 yards and dropped him with the first bullet. It sounds callous now, but at the time it was a case of you or them. We later discovered that it was this same gang which had chopped the head off the SAS man.

War is war, and if you are in a situation where others are out to kill you, for whatever reason, then the answer is to kill them first. It is a sad fact of life that has existed since time began. Kill or be killed.

We walked over to the Arab who was still alive, his arm blown off at the shoulder. He was bleeding to death, we could see that, so we packed the wound with a field dressing and buried his arm. At that moment the RSM appeared.

'What are you up to?' he asked.

'He's lost his arm and is dying, so we've buried it, RSM,' I replied.

'Then bloody unbury it!' he ordered. 'You'll be in trouble if you do things like that.'

So we dug it up again and strapped it to the dying man's chest. A helicopter came in and took him away to headquarters but soon after we heard on the radio that he had died. We all cheered. It sounds cruel and uncaring, but half an hour earlier he had tried to kill one of my mates.

We used to do many night marches, carrying water up from the valley, a march of about twenty-four miles, each carrying a jerry can weighing almost 50 lb apiece strapped to our backs. One night the bloke I was with strained his ankle badly so, for the last nine or ten miles, I carried two cans, a nasty load because the water slops about. For this effort I earned the name Sherpa McClean. I reckon I deserved it. When I was not called Sherpa, I was the Mountain Goat.

After we returned home to Aldershot we were each given a General Service Medal. The ridge where we had our little battle became known as Arnold's Ridge after the RSM, but has no doubt regained its old name now that the Yemeni people are running alongside the Russians. It was good to be home, taking leaves with the Venns and other friends and doing exercises in the English countryside.

It was at this time that I earned the nickname Moby, the one that stuck. It had nothing to do with my seafaring exploits that were to follow. Every so often the battalion padre would give us a pep talk on religion. I was at the back of the lecture room talking to a friend when a piece of chalk hit me on the head.

'If you don't stop spouting, Moby, I'll harpoon you next time,' he bellowed. The name stayed.

After less than a year at home we were off to Borneo to chase terrorists there. The SAS, again, had been there for some time working with the Royal Marines. Now it was our turn to try our hands at jungle fighting. I was coming up to twenty years old and loving every minute of army life. Our anti-tank platoon was once more disbanded and I was transferred into a scout company, based on the SAS style of operation: four men in a patrol, a commanding officer, a radio operator and two riflemen. We were to be based in Brunei, but were to be sent across the border into Borneo to look for communist infiltrators.

We started our tour of duty in Malaya for jungle training. This involved learning about jungle survival, ambushing in dense vegetation and other skills that we could not have learned in Britain. It suited me fine. Living off the land in that sort of country was my idea of heaven. Our headquarters in Brunei was an old wooden building which we called the Haunted House. It was from here that our scouting patrols were sent out into the border area by helicopter to spend a month, sometimes more, looking for terrorists.

We had the advantage as we patrolled our designated area, which was probably twenty miles square and stretched about five miles across the border into Borneo itself. It was one thing for four trained men to be there to listen and watch, quite another matter for the large enemy groups to try to cross the border and avoid us hearing or seeing them.

I had been transferred from rifleman and machine gunner

to signalman for the jungle operations, having been taught Morse and the use of special signalling equipment, coding and decoding signals. We made several patrols, being taken into our landing zone by a Royal Naval helicopter which would lower us into a clearing; we abseilled to the ground down a rope. The choppers never landed except under very rare circumstances as this would put them at risk from mines, ambush and other hazards. We would take food for a month, the familiar composite rations – compo – and bury most of it in a secret cache to which we would return for resupply. Extra ammunition, radio spares and medical kit would be hidden there as well.

Once our stores were safely hidden we set off on the first designated patrol. We never preplanned our route. There were many tricks to remember in order to survive, do our job and return to base safely. We never walked along river beds. The easiest way of trekking in the jungle is always the most dangerous. We used the thickest undergrowth and the most difficult climbs and descents. At night, to avoid insects and snakes, we slept in hammocks slung between trees, putting repellent round the base of each tree to deter trouble from climbing up. No one ever seemed to give much thought to insects and snakes coming down the trees at us, but none ever did so that must have been the reason.

We carried about five days' food with us. No smoking was allowed – before getting into the helicopter we were searched for cigarettes – because the smell of tobacco smoke in the jungle travels up to half a mile. We were also checked for metal mess tins. The sound of one of these clanking against another piece of equipment would carry as far as three miles on a still humid night. We took no soap or washing kit. No washing for three weeks; we smelled like jungle animals when we eventually returned home. Our weapons were different from those normally carried by the army. The lead scout had a Remington repeater shotgun which has a magazine of six cartridges. If he ever saw anything whatever, he would fire all six shots.

A typical day on jungle scouting patrol would start with the four of us standing to before dawn. We would quietly take positions facing the four corners of the compass, each with his quarter to watch. For up to two hours we would wait, watch and listen. No talking, no smoking, no brew of tea. Just silence, broken by the noises of the jungle waking. Many is the battle or military incident that has started at dawn so the action can benefit from the light of the day ahead. There is little action in the jungle at night because movement is virtually impossible in the total darkness. Even in daytime the umbrella of foliage which forms a roof overhead in the treetops makes the jungle dark and gloomy; at night no light from the moon or stars penetrates. It is total and complete blackness. Even the animals stop moving at night. They, like us, sleep, but with the dawn the whole place comes alive.

Once the dawn had broken and the awakening sounds of animals and birds had died down a little, it was time for breakfast. Two of the patrol would cook, while the other two kept lookout, known as 'stag' in the Paras. The patrol commander made a situation report on activities noticed, our plan for the day and other information. I, as the signaller, then coded it and sent it off on my radio to headquarters at Brunei, 300 miles away. We were then given the word to proceed. We set out slowly, cautiously, silently into the jungle. We seldom spoke, but used any of about seventy hand signals to communicate with one another.

The lead scout carried the lightest pack, whereas I, as the signaller, had the heaviest because I had to carry the radio as well as my own personal kit. Progress was boringly slow, about half a mile an hour. A few slowly and carefully made paces, then stop, listen, a few more paces, then stop again. We would move like this for an hour, then rest. Whenever we stopped we would crouch in a firing position, watching and listening to the many sounds of birds and occasional animals. Monkeys were a giveaway for anyone on the move, even the elephants, which we could hear crashing through the thick bush miles away. They always kept well away from us. Although we seldom saw animals we saw plenty of signs of them.

After a ten-minute break we moved off once more, four or five yards apart. At midday we stopped for coffee from flasks. One might imagine that because they came from the jungle the enemy were better than we were in the art of jungle warfare. Not true. The enemy, Indonesians, were hopeless, moving about talking, whistling and even playing transistor radios. They would stick to the tracks in groups of as many as eighty and we could hear them miles away. If we were on a recce patrol on the wrong side of the border we would hide and count the numbers as they went by. On one such patrol we hid a few yards off the track and I counted 112 men as they passed us. There was no point taking on a gang like that, but we reported their position, their direction and other details back to Brunei. We were the watchers. The fighting patrols, as many as a hundred men, were formed by Royal Marines or, more often than not, the Gurkhas.

Early in the evening we set up camp once more, but before that we would make figure-of-eight patrols to cover our tracks in case we were being tracked ourselves. We then selected our camp, never cutting a space. We never, ever, cut anything in the jungle. It would have been the quickest way of being found by the enemy.We did not even cut notches in trees to support the hammocks, which were made from khaki parachute panels and shroud lines. Each morning we rubbed earth into the places on the tree where the lines had been attached to cover up any bruising.

Weapons were always ready and within reach, even when we were having a crap, making tea or sleeping. Loaded, one bullet up the spout and the safety catch on. No cooking started until night, which comes early in that part of the world, had arrived. Before cooking we would take off our puttees and empty the leeches out of our trouser legs. These were little maggot-like insects which would attach themselves to the body and suck blood until they were the size of a respectable slug. Heat would get them off; just a touch from a stick or piece of metal heated on the cooker and the leech would drop off, head and all, a purple slug full of blood. It was dangerous to pull them off because the head would remain in your flesh and go septic.

We cooked in the dark on platforms of sticks so as not to leave signs of our cookers. It was a continual battle to ensure that there was never a sign of our presence in the area where we were operating.

It may seem odd that it was safe to light fires and cook at

night, but the enemy were scared of the jungle at night and would stay where they were. They thought that there were demons abroad at night. Perhaps, with us lurking about, they were right. We never made big fires, but enough to make a decent meal. A typical meal would be a curry bar with rice, finished off with a cup of tea and a biscuit. That was a real beano for us. It was hardly surprising when we came back off patrol that we had lost weight and were a deathly white owing to the lack of sun under the canopy of the tall trees above our heads. Only those back at base managed to get a good suntan.

By seven at night we were ready to settle for the night, ten hours' good sleep after a final hour of watching and listening. Next day, the same thing all over again. After a few days of this routine we would lose sense of days and weeks and slip into a timeless routine. For me this life was real soldiering. I enjoyed the close comradeship of the small group where everyone was responsible for the safety of everyone else. I did three or four patrols of three to four weeks until I caught tonsilitis and was sent to base hospital.

Having my tonsils taken out was far worse than any patrol and it took a little time to get fit again, probably because of the effects of the jungle which sapped some of my strength. I was taken off patrolling for a while and sent to Bareo where there was a large unit of Gurkhas, about two hundred of them. There I worked the radio for the patrols signalling in, passing the messages back to the Haunted House in Brunei. I should have been there for a couple of weeks but in fact stayed for eight.

Off duty I used to go down to the local kampong – village – and got to know the natives. I was asked into their long houses and came to know many of them very well. They looked wild, with pierced ears and noses, amazing hair styles and painted skin. Forty of them would live in each long house, the people upstairs and the animals underneath. There were two tribes, the Poonangs and the Dyaks, who both lived in the areas that we were patrolling. In spite of their fearsome appearance they were friendly and the younger ones became scouts, working alongside the British and Gurkha soldiers. One of them gave me a blowpipe with poisoned darts and a parang, a three-foot-long knife; I gave them a watch, which fascinated them, though it took them quite a while to understand that it showed the time of day. I also tried their local brew, a type of rice wine to which they would add strange things to sweeten it. It was kept in a big vat where it fermented for a few weeks. It became a gooey milky porridge-like mixture which you drank through a bamboo straw. It was very strong and could knock you out.

I think I was quite privileged because they invited me to go hunting with them for monkeys and birds, the natives using their blowpipes. They were nomads, travelling over the years through the jungle, moving on when the fruit and animals needed resting from the hunting. They hunted in groups of five men, wearing nothing except a loin cloth, no protection from leeches and insects. They each carried a bag for the game they killed and a bamboo holder for the deadly darts which they fired from the blowpipes.

To kill a monkey they would surround a tree where one or two monkeys would be sitting or scampering about and fire several of the poisoned darts at one of them. The first dart had little effect but after three or four more the monkey began to sway about on the bough. After a few minutes it dropped to the ground, to be grabbed and cut through in several places, with blood flowing rapidly everywhere. The loss of blood freed the body from the darts' poison, which, it seemed, simply stopped the heart by paralysing it. These nomads were a happy people with few cares in the world; no money, just barter, and living a day-to-day existence.

Some senior officers came down from Brunei to see how things were going at Bareo. They were a little concerned to find that Signaller McClean had gone native, the wild man of Borneo, dressed in a sarong, hunting with the locals and spending his free time in a long house. This, combined with my blowpipe, native sandals and almost every other native fashion except plaited hair and a pierced nose, made them wonder about me. Getting to know the locals was one thing, but they must have felt I had taken things a bit far.

Certainly the friendliness of the native people towards me had been infectious. I liked them and their interest in me. My ability to stalk, shoot and live in the jungle impressed them.

But all good things must come to an end and the bosses at headquarters decided that I needed bringing back into line so they hauled me back to the Haunted House in Brunei for further patrols. I was happy with this move. I had had my holiday and it was time to get back to the job.

We did several more scouting patrols and on one we became hopelessly lost. I am not sure how it happened as I was not the map reader, but we had been going a few days when the leader told us that we were lost. Instinctively I knew where we were, I do not know how, but I told them the way out and they left it to me. After two days I led them straight to the landing zone where the helicopter was to collect us and where our basic cache was hidden. I was almost as surprised as they were, but I had, and always have had, an excellent sense of direction. We made it, that was the main thing.

When lost in strange country you should always follow water down in the direction of the stream; that is a basic survival rule. All water ends at the sea and most main centres of help are based near rivers or on the coast. So is the enemy in hostile territory, so you must be careful. One day I want to go back to the jungle and see it again in less stressful conditions.

It was on one of our last three-week scouting patrols that we made a contact with the enemy and had to use our guns. Our leader saw something and opened up. We fired in the direction of his shots while backing off the way we had come. There were about thirty terrorists ahead, we later confirmed. We knew that someone was about and it was our job to find out who and how many.

They were a smaller enemy patrol than usual and were obviously more efficient than most because they certainly knew we were around. We made our separate ways back to our previous night's camp, which was standard procedure. I arrived to find no one else there. It had been a close call, but I was none the worse for it, slightly elated in fact, although I was alone. Progress back to camp had been slow, one minute moving very slowly, ten minutes waiting, listening. Thirty men looking for one sounds as though the odds should be in their favour, but it was the other way round. As long as I stayed calm and quiet I could hear them moving about. In the dense undergrowth it was possible to hide and watch the enemy searching around, sometimes only a few yards away. I was never frightened in the jungle. Excited, yes, but scared, never. I knew that we were better at the game than the opposition and it seemed that they knew that if they ever found one of us we would take more than a few of them with us so their searching was, perhaps, a little half-hearted. I think the Gurkhas had made them think like that, and we were not going to let the reputation already established by British forces be lessened.

I now had to make my way back to the landing zone alone. It had taken a week to get to where we met the enemy so it would take almost two to get back to the landing zone. Even then I would have to watch the area for a day or two to make sure that it had not been found and made into an ambush both for me and for the Royal Navy or Royal Marine pilots who would come and haul me out. They were great people, those pilots, taking more risks than they were ever given credit for, and they never let us down unless the situation was quite impossible. Even then they tried.

On my way back to the landing zone I had to live off the land. We had been trained in this, knowing what could be eaten and what should be avoided. Plants that look like the rubber trees one finds in British homes have an inside to the stalk which is like cabbage. I was in my element, remembering what the native people in the long houses had taught me as well as what I had learned from previous patrols and jungle training in Malaya. I made my way carefully, resting up at night, never going the shortest route, never moving for long without stopping to listen and sniff the air for the enemy. They were looking for me, so I had to keep one jump ahead.

I had the radio. The others had no way of contacting base, so each day I sent a quick blast of coded Morse reporting the situation as I read it, including the fact that the other three in our patrol had been separated. Brunei acknowledged the signals, but told me nothing. If I did not need to know something, they would not tell me the situation. A short sharp reply, 'Message received', was all I usually got. That was enough for me to know that I was on the right track.

For two days I stayed watching the landing zone, telling the people at headquarters what I was doing. None of the others appeared. Then, after a couple of days, there was the welcome sound, the chomping of the rotor blades as a helicopter came in to haul me and my radio pack with the other kit out of the jungle. Happiness.

The crewman in the cabin sniffed. 'Christ, you stink!' he said, with a smile.

'Yer!' I replied. 'It's my aftershave . . . Jungle Socks.'

The others trickled back to the landing zone over the next week and were brought back to the Haunted House for debriefing, a question and answer game in which the intelligence people found out what had been going on. It was then that I began to realize that I was something of a loner, a side of me that was going to help in the oceans later.

After Borneo, two six-month tours of patrols, we were taken out. It was considered a successful operation. The communist terrorists pulled out and peace and quiet returned to the land. It was, perhaps, something of a lesson to the Americans, who believed that tanks, guns and mighty armies could defeat an army of little people who can disappear in a twinkling of the eye into the local terrain. Such people must be taken on at their own game: local fighting, stealth, observation and befriending the people who live in the combat area, rather than bombing them indiscriminately with napalm. Respect, whether from the friendly natives or from the enemy, is worth a thousand bullets and many lives. If the enemy can survive for weeks, even months, living in holes in the ground, then we have to learn to do the same, but better.

I was sent home to Blighty for a spell. Then the same sort of trouble brewed up on the Thai border with Malaya. Infiltrators. Communist terrorists trying to disrupt the local villages, sapping the food and supplies, attempting to spread their ideas farther afield. We were back to the four-men patrols. It was like Borneo all over again, but the girls in the villages were prettier, no ears a foot long with weights, and no long houses with animals underneath.

After about six uneventful months patrolling in Malaya we

were sent home once more. I only had a few more months to do to complete the term for which I had originally signed on, so I came out, thinking that it was time to try my arm in civvy street. It was not long, working on building sites, before I wished I had stayed in the army. Perhaps, I thought, I should join the Special Air Service. Plenty of people in the Paras had talked about it and quite a few had joined. One morning, instead of going to work, I decided to try for the SAS, my way. Normally one transfers from the army, which would have meant my rejoining the regiment and starting from there.

I could not be bothered with this idea, so I climbed into the old Bedford van which I now owned and drove down to the SAS depot at Hereford. I arrived at the main gate guard room, told them who I was and that I wanted to see the commanding officer. They were a bit surprised and told me that I had to have a proper interview and an appointment. But when they realized that I was not going to leave they began making a few telephone calls round the base. To my relief I was told that the CO, Colonel John Slim, would see me that evening. (Colonel Slim was the son of Field Marshal Sir William Slim, one of Britain's leading soldiers in the Second World War.)

He told me that no one could join the regiment straight from civilian life. However, as I had managed to get into the depot and because of my service record, I could attend the next selection course. That was two months away so, happy as a kid with credit at the sweetshop, I went home to train and get myself really fit.

3 Who Dares Wins

There seems to be some confusion in the minds of the public about the SAS and what it does. It had developed from the days when it was first formed in North Africa by David Stirling. Then anyone who wanted to work as a behind-the-lines man could join. They needed to be able to parachute, have imagination, be very fit and have an inbuilt will to survive. Later, as war became more specialized, so did the SAS. Today it is a highly technical regiment.

One hundred and five men arrived at Hereford to take the selection course and only three passed, one officer and two soldiers. I was one of them. It was not as tough as I had thought it would be; it was more a question of attitude. Fitness was important. The course started with a forced march of about thirty-five or forty miles, carrying a pack of 66 lb loaded with painted bricks, a nasty concentrated load but nothing for the Mountain Goat. There were various check-points where the packs were weighed to make sure we had all the bricks still aboard.

The whole course, right from the start, was an individual business. You were on your own, no one to team up with, share decisions or share the load, whatever load, mental or physical, was applied. During and between exercises and schemes we lived rough, sleeping under our capes. No tents, no cover. We were watched the whole time. Our conversations were listened to, discreetly, and a slip meant instant failure. As we were loading into a transport for the next exercise, one bloke, a good man, who was always up front during the forced marches, simply said, 'Here we bloody well go again.' Thirty minutes later he was given a travel warrant to his unit.

What they were looking for were fit, keen young men who were determined to be real soldiers, determined to survive, not to be broken by pressure and, most important, able to do all this entirely on their own. During the first week of the course thirty men left for various reasons, some of their own choice, others being given the travel warrant, a pat on the back for effort and thanks from the SAS for coming. After that the failure rate decreased, dropping to around ten per week for the next fortnight. At the beginning of the fourth week, with half the original starters still in the chase, we were tested at escape and evasion. This exercise lasted a whole week, most of it out on our own, navigating from one checkpoint to the next. Failure at navigation did not necessarily mean failing on the course, but lack of drive and initiative certainly did. A few fell by the wayside here.

Next, interrogation. Four days of torment. I was put in a dark hole, pitch black in fact, wearing just my underpants, and sprayed with a cold hose. There was only artificial light so I had no idea whether it was night or day. All this after the week of escape and evasion. The guards wore foreign uniform. They dragged us into the interrogation room and they were really rough. They would thump you with a pick handle, physically hit you, trying to provoke a reaction. The questioning was severe. The interrogators would ask about family, school, girlfriends, anything. They seemed to know everything about us. They would suggest that your girlfriend or wife, whom they knew by name, was carrying on with a pal. They would give his name and a whole load of accurate details.

After an hour or more of questions, with me sitting there in wet underpants, they would say, 'OK, McClean, off you go for a hot shower and we'll chat again in an hour.' Relax.

No sooner was I out of the door, thinking of that shower, than three guards gave me a real hammering, blacking an eye, bruising my ribs and kicking me in the crutch. Then I was sprayed with more cold water and put in a forty-gallon oil drum, with air holes halfway up the side and the bottom covered with rotten animal offal. The lid was slammed shut and I was left there for, I guess, about a day and a half. The only distraction was a piercing whistle that blew every so often for long periods. It destroyed all thought and concentration and made my head sing with almost physical pain.

Apart from the mental and physical discomfort, which was part of the selection procedure, there was the added element of degradation, or that was what it was intended to be. During one of the interrogation periods, when I was at a fairly low ebb, again the promise of a hot shower, dry towel and clean clothes was made. I answered the questions and headed for the door indicated to me by one of the interrogators. I walked through into a dark space and then on through a further door. Opening this, I found I was in a plain white windowless room where another guard ordered me to strip, which I did. He then left.

A few moments later three women came in, large and none too pretty. They stood looking at me.

'Look what we've got here!' said one. 'That wouldn't be much fun for a girl like me on a Saturday night after a party.'

She was staring at me with a teasing grin. It was one of the few times I lost my cool.

'If it was you I had to spend a Saturday night with I wouldn't be bothered trying. I expect an ugly old bird like you has to pay for it.'

It worked, just. The other two, almost as unappealing as the first, were laughing, not at me now, but at her. She was furious. Two points to McClean. They left, but not after a few more insults. I never saw them again.

Another little test that must have been thought up by some demon was, again, partly degrading and partly a trial of one's reaction to totally repulsive surroundings. Once more the large oil drum was used. I was placed in it either naked or just in a pair of underpants. It made little difference.

Again the bottom was about nine inches deep in what seemed to be rotting offal – old bits of liver, lights, sweetbreads, slime, or even worse. That was bad enough for a sensitive chap like me, but every so often, maybe once an hour, sometimes longer, the whole thing would be turned upside down. The result was a shower of whatever was in the bottom of the drum. Disorientated by the darkness and cold, I struggled to find my feet and emerged, covered in the filth, in a standing position once more, to await the next capsize.

Bits of the stinking slime clung to my hair and found its way into my mouth as I fought for breath. It even filled my nose and ears. Shutting my eyes tightly as the drum began to turn over helped keep them reasonably free from the muck. I found that forcing tears also washed my eyes clear after a few moments. Those sessions of torture, for they were nothing more, nothing less, were interspersed with more interrogations, more nasty surprises and letdowns, but I battled on, determined to pass the selection procedure. I often spoke to myself out loud, carefully choosing my words in case my surroundings were bugged by hidden microphones, as I was almost certain was the case.

'Come on, Moby, don't react. Keep calm, think. It's only a game!'

Physical reaction to the beatings would only bring more, and probably failure as well. The answer was to hang on as long as you could. Give nothing away. The idea was to try to find out if you could keep your mouth shut. This might mean that in action, if captured, you would be able to hold out until any information wanted by a real enemy was out of date if and when you eventually cracked. I don't know whether I would have cracked, but I managed to hold out. That, for the moment, was enough.

The interrogation lasted for four and a half days, I discovered when it ended. I was bruised, battered, damp but unbowed, and I passed. I was awarded the famous khaki brown beret with the winged dagger badge and posted to 'D' Squadron as a trooper. It was now 1967 and we were sent to Guyana for jungle training.

Not long after we arrived in Guyana I was bitten on the back of the neck by a poisonous snake. The medical orderly, who should have given me a pill to slow my pulse after the antiserum injection, gave me a booster pill by mistake. My pulse rate soared to 180 beats a minute. It was an amazing sensation, as if all the adrenaline in my body was on the move at the same time. I was marched out, five miles, to the first-aid post, where I met Major Hedges again, the doctor who had operated on me after I had been shot in Greece. He prescribed some more pills and two days' rest before sending me back to continue training.

We then returned to Hereford where I was put into the squadron's boat troop, a troop of twenty men. Each trooper had a special skill: boating, climbing, freefall parachuting or some other personal best trick. My skill, apart from boating, was, as in the Paras, wireless operator, working the 128 set. We brushed up on other skills as well: driving Land Rovers in rough country, parachuting at night, survival, and night navigation by map.

During one exercise we were up in the Brecon Beacons in the Welsh hills, acting as escapers being hunted by other troops. It was snowing hard and getting dark. I found some fertilizer bags, big plastic ones, and made trousers and a waistcoat out of them, covered myself with some more, and lay down. By morning a good two feet of snow had fallen and I was completely buried. I was about to start moving but first, as trained, I listened out for sounds. Someone was coming, so I lay quite still. A whole patrol of searching soldiers went right by without seeing me, only five yards away.

It was 1968 and the world seemed to have gone quiet from an active soldier's point of view. Borneo had ended with high praise being showered down from the bosses above, we were out of Malaya, and elsewhere things were peaceful. The problems in Northern Ireland had yet to begin. We went to Norway for an exercise with the Royal Marines, using Gemini inflatable raiding boats. We were dropped in the sea about fifteen miles out. It was a very rough night landing and my first time at sea in a small boat. I loved it.

The quiet period in my life as a soldier, apart from the occasional exercise, reawakened thoughts of rowing the Atlantic single-handed. I had first got the idea while I was still in the Paras, serving in the Far East. In the newspapers that had filtered out to us I had seen stories that John Ridgway and Chay Blyth were going to attempt a transatlantic crossing, which they did, in 1966. My joining the SAS had meant that schemes for voyages such as this had to be shelved. It was only later, during those quieter times and after the boat training with the SAS, that the ideas began to take shape. I had already started to make plans, however.

Training continued and I joined in, but when time allowed my main priority was the voyage. I was learning to speed up transmitting Morse, but my thoughts were continually drifting off to what lay ahead.

4 The Atlantic, the Ultimate Challenge

It was in 1966 that John Ridgway and Chay Blyth achieved the feat of rowing across the Atlantic. Later that year, back at SAS headquarters in Hereford, various members of the regiment were preparing schemes with a difference. Two friends were planning to walk across the United States, others were plotting expeditions. Me? My thoughts were on the Atlantic.

Several of my SAS friends thought that Chay and John were mad, but I stuck up for them as I knew otherwise. John Ridgway had been my platoon commander in the Paras, and Chay had been platoon sergeant. In the barrack room at Hereford I opened my big mouth as usual. I announced that I thought a man could make the crossing of the Atlantic, from Canada to Europe, alone.

'Belt up, Moby,' my companions said. 'You're bloody bats. It took Blyth and Ridgway all their time to do it together, and, as they told us, it was no picnic.'

I didn't say anything at the time but kept my thoughts to myself. I was convinced that with the right boat, proper planning and enough determination I could make the voyage and win a record for Britain, a first so far as I knew. I would need some luck, but other factors were more important. That same day I started by writing off to the suppliers of Admiralty charts for details of the Canadian and European coasts, and for Atlantic charts showing tides and currents that I would need to plan the route. Ireland or Scotland seemed to be the place to aim for, but I would have to decide that when I was once at sea.

The suppliers could not understand why a member of the SAS should ask, privately, for these charts. Being responsible to the services and closely associated with the Ministry of Defence, they took it upon themselves to contact my regiment. Perhaps they thought I was planning to desert or start a private war. Some weeks after sending off my list of requests I was summoned to the office of my squadron commander, Major Dodds.

'Now then, McClean,' he asked rather abruptly, 'what's all this business about Atlantic charts?'

As I have frequently been told, I am a person who is inclined to speak before thinking. Now, as I stood there, the whole plan seemed to come alive.

'I want to row the Atlantic, sir.'

'Alone?' asked Major Dodds. His face was a picture. I almost burst out laughing but managed to contain myself.

'Yes, sir. Alone. It can be done.'

The major continued to stare at me for almost a minute, his eyes moving slowly up and down all 5 foot 6½ inches of me. Finally he coughed and said, 'You're mad, McClean. Are you absolutely sure? Do you realize just what such a project is going to entail?'

'Yes, sir,' I said again.

'Right,' he replied. 'You seem to have made up your mind, so I'll fix an interview for you with the CO.'

In the early part of 1967 I was called to an interview with Colonel John Slim. He was very direct in his questioning, being neither for nor against my plan. First he wanted to be sure that I was certain I wanted to do it, that it was not just a burst of 'Moby thinking' which had gone out of control. Having assured himself that I meant to go, he made a few initial facts clear. I was to decide on what sort of boat I needed, try some long-distance rowing at sea and talk to Ridgway and Blyth.

I had already decided that the dory-type of boat was ideal, if there was an ideal boat. I went to the Isle of Wight, hired a heavy clinker-built boat and rowed around the Solent for eight hours, nonstop. The McClean body worked; SAS training had ensured that. The brain had received similar training, so I could see no problem in coping with the mental struggle that lay ahead.

Next I took a train to the far north of Scotland to visit John Ridgway at his new adventure school that he and his wife Marie-Christine had started to run from a croft at Ardmore, twenty miles south of Cape Wrath. I had always respected him and his way of doing things in the army, but he took the wind out of my sails. First, he doubted that any man could make the crossing on his own. There had been moments when he and Chay, together, had had their doubts that they would survive. He then told me that I would need two or three years to prepare, build the boat and set off from Newfoundland. I headed south again, feeling deflated, on my way to see Chay Blyth at his home near Portsmouth.

Three years – sod that, I thought, but I knew that Ridge had to lay it on the line. It was not the moment to paint pretty pictures when a project like this lay ahead.

Chay really bucked me up. He thought it was a great idea, feasible and exciting, but pointed out the risks. Certainly he had no doubt that it could be done, probably by someone with a background such as he, Ridge and I shared, training in the Paras and the SAS, but he spelt out the odds. He gave me an 80–20 chance of making it – four to one; not bad odds, I reckoned.

Chay's wife, Maureen, impressed me. I wondered how wives put up with the sort of behaviour that drives us to these mad schemes. Then, I thought, with no wife, not even a steady girlfriend, and no family, there was one problem I didn't have to bother about.

I reported back to Colonel Slim who contacted the Ministry of Defence. They gave permission for me to make the trip, granting me paid leave for the time needed to make the preparations and unpaid leave while I was actually rowing. That should spur me along across the Atlantic. So, into battle.

Bradford Boat Services had built *English Rose III* for John and Chay so they should be good enough for me. I had £200 in my savings to pay for a boat and would need £3000 to finance the whole business of the crossing. As word of my plans got around help appeared. Chay had advised me to find an agent so I asked Paul Sargent to help. He had recently been picture editor of the *Daily Mail* until his sight began to fail, forcing him to retire, but he had set up a successful business as agent for all sorts of people. He soon had the wheels rolling and help came from many quarters.

The boat was bought and moved to the carpenter's shop at the SAS Hereford headquarters. It was April 1969 and Ridge's three years were looking a little lost from sight. Nearer two, I thought.

Buoyancy compartments were fitted, with water tanks under the floor, the idea being that if the boat turned over, the weight of water would right her, helped by the polystyrene packed in the side compartments. I was to be glad of those tanks. They saved my neck twice. Gillette had promised help and the *Sunday Express* offered to buy my log books and film, paying a sum before I started and the rest when I arrived. I could now afford to go. The boat was named *Super Silver*, after a Gillette razor blade being launched on the market at that time, though the boat became known to me simply as *Silver*.

Food supplies were a problem, but the army helped, providing a hundred SAS field ration packs, each containing enough to support one man in action for one day. I knew all about those, I should say so!

We were nearly ready. Furness Withy had offered to ship the boat and stores to St John's in Newfoundland free of charge. I was to fly over on an RAF Comet which was taking personnel to the RAF base at Goose Bay. Everything was packed and my basic navigation equipment aboard. I had taken a crash course in ocean navigation, just enough to take a sextant fix, but with my ability at maths, it was still something of a bugger's muddle in my mind. The main thing, I reckoned, was to keep going east. I was bound to hit Europe somewhere and then I could sus out where I was by asking. It sounded easy and, in fact, that's just what happened.

I reached St John's early in May 1969. The Royal Canadian Mounted Police, the Mounties, gave me free accommodation in their barracks and canteen, and people invited me into their homes like a long-lost relative. The boat was already there but the Canadian Customs Authority were refusing to release it from bond. After two days of frustration and worry I managed to persuade a customs officer to slide back the doors of the warehouse in which *Silver* was imprisoned. I stuck my head through the gap and could see the boat carefully placed on stacks of matting and covered by canvas tarpaulins. I couldn't have done better myself, but I needed to get going. Frustration was mounting. I went for runs and walks, visited the place from where Marconi had sent his original transatlantic radio signal, and was asked by a Mountie if I wanted to go to church. Me? Church?

Suddenly I understood. He thought that anyone about to row the ocean might want to pray; in fact he bloody well ought to pray. I made the excuse that I did not have the right clothes, but that did not deter him. Most Mounties are at least 6 feet tall, but he said he would find me a suit. An hour later he had fitted me out in a suit of a man 2 inches taller than I was. The trousers had to be rolled up at the ankles, but my top half, thanks to the training of HM the Queen, filled the jacket fairly well.

We set out for the church with Harold Squires, a local civil servant, and it was the start of a friendship that still holds well. Harold and his family took me in as one of them, and while his wife Jean fussed about me, their children, Elizabeth, Robin, Ann, Jean and David, adopted me as a new brother. It was a good feeling, just what I needed to keep my mind off my imprisoned boat. I prayed in church, asking God to get me on my way. The next time I was to pray was in mid-ocean. I meant it on both occasions, for different reasons.

Two days later my prayers seemed to have been answered: the boat was released from bond by the customs. I wondered whether Harold had a hand in this, but didn't ask. The appearance of *Silver* caused quite a stir in the harbour, the home of the famous Newfoundland Banks dories on which she was modelled. In spite of this, the natives, although remaining friendly, thought I was mad; of this I was sure, though no one actually said anything.

The chippies at Hereford had painted the SAS emblem on the bow of the boat so I felt more at home already. Three local teenagers, Glen and John Allen and Michael Guihan, helped load the stores and stow them in the various nooks and crannies in the boat. Even in St John's it was thought that there should be a guard on such a vulnerable boat at night. I said that I would sleep aboard but the kids would hear nothing of that; I needed all the sleep I could get, they insisted. They mounted two-hour watches on the boat, even attracting the attention of a passing Mountie, who took some convincing that they were about legal business in the early dawn. Such was the spirit of the place.

Another helper was Ed Gedden, Big Ed, paymaster of Furness Withy in St John's. He was a hard critic and watched the loading with a professional eye. Then he asked about my gloves. Gloves? I had two pairs, one woollen and the other leather.

'Useless,' he growled. 'You might as well have none in that cold out there. What you need is Portuguese fishermen's gloves. Wool soaked in cod oil. Used out on the Banks. They last for ever and when you get them wet, just wring them out, put them back on and they'll still keep your hands warm. I'll get you some.'

He did, and I have them yet, a little worn, but still in use at Ardintigh where I live now.

Saturday, 17 May: the moment of truth. The previous night I had had supper with the Squires family. David had asked me how I felt. 'Just like I did before my first parachute jump,' I told him. As I went to bed that night, my last night in a house for many weeks, I thought about his question. If there was only a four to one chance of surviving a parachute jump, then people would have to be mad to try it.

A big breakfast and off to the boat. Half the world and his wife were there to see me go: cameramen, Peter Vane from the *Sunday Express*, who was covering my trip, fishermen, and half the population of St John's. Many friends. I could live in Canada, I thought. Someone handed me a girlie magazine, someone else a bottle of whisky. 'Christen the boat with that,' a voice called out, and I did just that, cracking the bottle over the bow. There was not a dry eye on the jetty after that little gesture, in a place where whisky is currency. Finally I sat on the thwart, pushed out the oars and took the first strokes towards the open sea. I watched the faces, sure that some of them were certain that I would never be seen again. Time to be off, of that I was now sure.

Fishing boats were still with me through the treacherous narrows at the entrance of the harbour. I had been told to keep rowing away from the coast as fast as I could out into the open sea, so I rowed for twelve hours straight. I had to get out of the coastal current that could sweep me back onto the rocky shoreline. I only stopped for some tea in the afternoon, from a thermos given to me by the Squires, and to be sick, very sick. It was due partly to the nasty swell and partly to release from the tension that had built up ashore.

The Atlantic gave me a right welcome. First, the cold, a misty breeze that managed to penetrate everywhere and everything. Next, blisters on my hands. I had trained on wallbars, branches of trees and in boats, but the days since leaving Britain had softened me. There were already three blisters on each hand, big watery lumps that made the oars feel enormous. A fresh northwesterly wind was piping up as I decided to resort to basic surgery. I bit through each blister with my eye teeth, squeezing out the fluid and then dipping my hand in a bucket of sea water. Christ, it hurt, but desperate problems need desperate treatment. I pickled the skin in brine, forming a hard layer of padding. The oars felt normal again and I rowed on.

The first few days were a real baptism of fire. Sore hands, cold feet, some sleep curled up in the bottom of the boat. At night frost formed on the entire upper surface of the boat. I saw whales and thought of friends at home. John and Pauline Venn seemed very close. Perhaps I really wanted to be back on the farm. My first storm came at the end of the first week. Fifty-knot icy winds and seas that dumped water in the boat every ten minutes or so. I pumped for my life, ignoring the pain in my hands. If this is summer in the Atlantic then next time I'll row the Indian Ocean, I thought. Sod this for a joke, and I'm not even being paid for it. Pay stopped last week until I get home. The army knows a trick or two. I couldn't row in rough seas; the oars kept being snatched by the waves. Although I had spares, this was not the time to lose one, so I huddled in the boat and pumped out water, occasionally munching at a ration pack.

The other problem, apart from the blisters, was the cold. I had to eat to keep warm, food providing that warmth when it was too rough to keep warm by rowing. Pumping used energy, and the pump was hardly coping with all the water flying into the boat. I resorted to a five-gallon bucket, but having to maintain my balance while shifting as much as forty gallons a minute was backbreaking work.

Then my feet began playing up. A dull pain filled my seaboots, which had not been off for more than a week. It had taken me several days to find my sea legs and establish something of a routine; now my real legs were cracking up. I decided to wait for the weather to ease before taking off my boots and socks; in fact I would peel off the two sets of underwear, shirts, jerseys, double oilskins and the rest and have a real sortout once the wind and sea allowed. A good general clean – and brush my teeth. I read some crap somewhere that the SAS don't use toothpaste or brush their teeth when in ambush or on patrol. Nonsense. We don't use toothpaste because it smells. We use sand or mud, or nothing, just the brush. The smell of toothpaste wouldn't matter out here. I wondered where it was stowed. Luxury, clean teeth. McClean teeth, my little joke.

The freezing weather continued for ten days as I crossed the Labrador current that sweeps down into the Atlantic from between Greenland and Canada to meet the Gulf Stream, causing the famous fogs over the Newfoundland Banks. The winds stayed with me and I rowed about eight hours a day. My hands had hardened. Hell, I thought, I'm going to be a right little killer when this lot's over.

The weather and cold eased when I was eleven days out from Canada. It was time to examine the feet. I found a book, *A Traveller's Guide to Health*, by Lieutenant Colonel James Adam of the Royal Army Medical Corps. My bible on health matters, it turned out. It seemed that I had frostbite and should apply my feet to the abdomen of a colleague. Good old Colonel Adam, he hadn't reckoned on a para being alone in the Atlantic suffering from trench foot and frostbite when he wrote that paragraph. Massage and clean dry socks were the answer, so I rubbed away until both feet hurt and tingled. Then I put on dry pairs of socks of oiled wool and pulled my boots over the top. Round these I wrapped plastic dustbin liners used for stowing food and taped them to my legs with army tape. Dry warm feet were a great improvement, but in the cold weather and storms I had developed salt sores in every crease and crinkle of my body, and I mean every crease. Some were really sore, especially the old area of the wound where that bloody idiot had shot me through the groin. That part was all right, but the scar on my bum, where the bullet had done so much damage, was causing a bit of strife. If only the doctors and nurses from the Cambridge could see me now.

Sleeping in the cold was not too bad. I rolled into a bundle under the covers in my sleeping bag on the airbed, my only real concession to luxury. I would cup my hands over my face and breathe into the sleeping bag, recirculating the warmth created in my lungs. Arctic training can be useful, even in mid-Atlantic.

At one point I almost fell out of the boat hunting for a broken curry-paste jar and a food pack. It had been a near thing, the boat being hit by an awkward wave while I was off balance, but I managed to hang on. The worst of it, apart from the shock, was getting soaked from the waist upwards. From then on I decided to wear a lifeline attached to the boat, but not a lifejacket.

Why bother? If I fell overboard and the lifeline broke I would have two choices. Swim like hell for the boat or drown. A lifejacket would impede a fast swimmer. A slow swimmer, lifejacket and all, would drown, the lifejacket just dragging out the business of dying. Death itself has never really worried me, and I've seen a lot of it, but when my turn comes I want it as quick as possible, not drawn out like a bad B movie. Pow! Zapped out . . . gone.

At the end of May I hit the edge of the warmer weather and the Gulf Stream sweeping its way northeastwards from Florida and the Gulf of Mexico. Warmer, bluer water, a change from the grey lumpy sludge from the north. And the sun came out. I fiddled around with navigation but, to be quite honest, although it was a good idea, there was very little in the way of results. The only thing in common with McClean and maths is that they both start with the letter M.

With the sun, the whole project took on a different feeling. Dry clothes, calmer seas, so I could cook a really good hot meal: beef curry and rice. My hands, still sore in places, had a chance to dry out without the mittens.

Before leaving home I had been given a bundle of letters by friends. They were to be opened on Sundays, one or two a weekend, and were stowed aboard in a screw-topped plastic box. That sunny Sunday I opened a letter from Val and June, girls on the telephone switchboard at Hereford. It was a real shot in the arm. They asked that God should keep me safe and hoped that Pinky the elephant was still aboard. Pinky the elephant? Where the hell was it? God had done his bit so far, but where was Pinky? Panic. I rushed about the boat looking in corners, but it was not until the next day that I found him, tucked away in a container with my fishing gear. Relief! You stupid sod, McClean, you'll be crying in your beer next! But I spent an hour nailing mascots given to me by wellwishers along the top of the dodger – a St Christopher, a one cent piece given to me by a Newfoundlander . . . and Pinky.

No sooner had I done this, surveying the little row of mascots as I rowed, when the next storm struck. What a howler. *Silver* and I bounced about all night, with me tucked under the dodger and spray cover, jammed against the RAF life raft and the cooker, listening to the wind howling above trying to tear us to pieces.

That night I prayed. 'Please God, help me see this through, help me fight this storm.' It helped. Next day the storm dropped as quickly as it had arrived, but I was exhausted after a night of humping, pumping and the desolate wetness that was everywhere. In the morning, as the wind dropped, I noticed that bits of seaweed were hanging all over the boat. Sargasso weed from the ocean to the south, I hoped, not from land to the west. I had to find out where I was.

I was rowing slowly, wondering where all the ships had gone, when suddenly I saw one. It was miles away, toylike in the distance, but I hopped about, waving my arms and shouting. Would it stop? Would they offer me fresh food, a bath, a bed? Would I accept these luxuries? I didn't know the answer, but I was to be put to the test in a few hours. Meanwhile the ship steamed away, out of sight, leaving me as flat as a rotten tyre. I turned on my radio, still able to hear St John's and the news of the great world beyond my ocean. No mention of me, so perhaps they thought I was safe. Hope so. It never occurred to me to think that I may already have been given up for lost. A mist swept over the water, and between periods of rowing I sat propped on the dinghy thinking of home.

Suddenly, right behind me in the light mist, a bell was ringing. There, not two hundred yards away, was a ship, a big ocean-going trawler with people lining the rails shouting and waving. I waved back as the ship drew alongside.

'Anythink you vant?' called the skipper from the bridge wing. 'You vant help, food, rescue? You OK?'

'Just my position, I'm fine,' I called back, waving my chart. Suddenly the ship's engines opened up and she steamed off.

'Damn!' I said aloud. But the ship was moving clear to pull in her trawl. This done, she circled round and came alongside once more, the skipper there again. The ship was the *Rio Alfusqueiro*, probably from Portugal.

'You are at 46 degrees 54 minutes north, 47 degrees 24 minutes west. Maybe you want food, water?'

'No thanks, just that position. Many thanks,' I called back, deliberately pushing the oars out and starting to row east. The crew waved the Churchill salute, the right way round, and the ship slowly dropped from sight as they shot their trawl again. I felt great, better than for days, as I plotted the position on my chart. I was 350 miles from St John's, in the Gulf Stream. Seventeen days out, twenty miles a day, or an average of about one and a half miles an hour. I was out of the really cold conditions and was happy that the first part of the voyage had been tough because it had broken me into the business right from the start, but I felt sure that with almost 2000 miles still to go there were more surprises in store for me. How right I was.

For the next three days I made good progress to the east, helped by west winds and reasonable seas. Given my average so far, I still had a hundred days to go, but the Gulf Stream, which sweeps along at up to 2 knots even out in the ocean, would help cut that by a lot – at least I hoped that would be the case.

Salt sores were a problem. They were very bad. I prepared a kettle of warm fresh water and stripped off, letting the sun get to my body while I dabbed at the worst bits, wiping the congealed salt and broken skin away. Then I sunbathed. I should have been rowing, but I felt the sun was doing more good than the fresh water. I dozed and dreamed that my pals at Hereford – the Horse, Nick and Lofty – were circling the boat in a Gemini rubber assault craft bringing a two-dozen-bottle crate of beer. They climbed aboard, I took a beer and opened it. Then I woke up. I was cold, shivering. The sun had been replaced by that Labrador mist. I was hallucinating. I was slipping, that I knew.

The medics had warned me about this before I set out and it had been part of the SAS training, particularly when operating for a long time with little food and warmth. Watch out for the signs of losing your grip. I pulled on my clothes, brewed some hot tea and then set about the oars, forcing the blood round my body. I even managed a smile when I remembered my dream, plodding on at the oars. In . . . out . . . in . . . out . . . I was warm once more, but had to be careful. Every day took a little more out of my reserves and there were plenty more days ahead. I was still tired but kept rowing, going into the 'marching doze', a skill taught in the army. Not exactly taught, but acquired; a half-sleeping condition into which one slips while doing a long slog with a 120-lb pack across rough country, now popularly known as a 'yomp'. I did a rowing yomp, my mind about 2000 miles from my body, my body pulling and heaving mechanically as I subconsciously slept. It worked at sea, but it was a dangerous state and I had to snap out of it once more. A hot fresh-water shave was the answer, and the magic tooth brush.

It became cold again, with the mist once more sweeping from the northwest. Oh God, I thought, I'm being swept back into the Labrador current, northwards away from Ireland, even Scotland. Maybe I would fetch up in Norway or Iceland. All the flotsam of the Atlantic washes ashore in those northern countries, but I was determined not to become part of it. Shaving was a disaster, though I had to keep quiet about that later when I met my co-sponsors, Gillette. Not their fault, mine, for leaving my beard to grow for two weeks before trying a new blade on a salt-sore face. It was a massacre, blood everywhere. Lethargy still prevailed. I didn't know why and was too dozy to sit down and think it out, though I recognized the danger signs. My reactions were slowing, however hard I tried to press on, and I fought it. I remembered John Ridgway's advice. 'You've got the physical strength, Moby,' he had said, 'but when it comes to the real crunch, it all depends on the mind. It's in the mind.' Pressure, but the pressure, one of Ridge's favourite words, is always in the mind if the body can cope. Luckily, though still cold, the sea was calm, undemanding. Maybe I needed a storm to sort me out.

Then, on Sunday, 8 June, I took my lucky dip in the letter box and pulled out a letter from Major Woods, the unit education officer. Positive thinking was his theme. He may have despaired of me as a potential scholar, but he knew me as a person for all that. Positive thinking . . . no shirkers, that was the SAS cry. Then a fog swirled in to replace the mist, a real fog. It must have been the edge of the cold water meeting the wandering Gulf Stream again. I hoped so and rowed doggedly onwards, trying to be more positive. Then the needed crunch came. *Bang*. The whole boat lurched as if hit by a hammer. I could see nothing. Fear gripped me, not for the first time in that extraordinary loneliness, exaggerated by the clammy mist.

Had I been hit? By what? I looked about. No driftwood or floating wreckage from another ship. A whale? I shall never know, but the moment put me into action, adrenaline running at 100 m.p.h. I was afloat, alive and working at maximum stretch. No holes, but was the hull damaged? In the dark – it was night time – and the mist, I examined the inside of the hull with my torch. All seemed well.

Tomorrow, I thought as I snuggled down for a few hours' kip before dawn, I would have to look at the bottom of the boat from the outside. A wet head if ever there was one, a prospect I didn't relish when I felt the scars on my face, the result of my shaving and the sea. I'll tell you one thing now, the aftershave for the toughest chap is sea water. It may not catch the birds, but it surely sorts out the men from the boys.

Dawn broke, thick fog trying to cheat the sun if there was

one. I prepared for the dip, brewing tea and making a sort of porridge from the oatmeal cakes in the ration pack. Strength. I would need it. As the world's worst swimmer, I had to pull myself together. Coward McClean, I shouted to the fog. Over you go.

I tied my lifeline round the solid samson post near the bow, took three deep breaths and went head first over the side. Shit, it was cold – and there was another thought: I had not had one for about four days. Who was it who said that a blocked-up body and mind were equally dangerous? I think it was an ocean-racing man, Captain John Illingworth, in a yachting book I had read, lent to me by someone before the start of this trip. Anyway, whoever, he was right. It was probably all part of the general lack of Press On. After the epic dive it would be the epic crap. Clear the mind, clear the body – that was the order of things.

Swearing, except when letting off surplus steam, is not part of me nowadays, but it was then. It was so cold that I muttered a few choice phrases to myself as I did a parallel-bar roll and looked at the port side of the hull. All was well.

I surfaced and struggled and clambered aboard, looking for the rest of my tea. God, it was cold, that sea. A man might last ten minutes in that according to the book, and I was going to survive. Who dares wins. It really did mean something. I was going to win, but first I had to look at the other side of the boat. In again, upside down, head down, gulping sea water, struggling to keep my eyes open in the cold, I looked at the starboard side. No cracks or holes showed. Just a few gooseneck barnacles which I ripped off. Cold. Shackleton would have been proud of me, and, after all, he was my hero. Only my feet, still in their plastic bags, were dry and warm.

I dressed again, made some cocoa as a dawn treat and sat thinking. The dip had done my head, my thoughts, good. I listened to a service from a church at St John's on my radio. All those good people would be there, those good people, as good as any I had known, who might, some of them, even be praying for me as they sat in their warm little church. It's often, they say, that a man alone finds God. Certainly being alone helped me to come to understand what the people at

Fegans had tried to tell us with their three visits to church every Sunday. On the other hand, perhaps God, or whoever, understood that a twelve-year-old mind finds it a bit much to cope with religion when survival was number one. Survival was number one then, in mid-ocean, but I never asked him to help, I just submitted my request, like when I asked the colonel, John Slim, if I could do the trip. He was, so far as I was concerned, God then; now he had a deputy.

Enough philosophy! Especially from a man who reckoned that the best thing to come from a church was the lead and copper from the roof. Maybe God knew about that but still saw some good in me, or maybe he was waiting round the corner with a great sledgehammer, ready to get his own back. Like maths, God is a muddling business, enough to send me back to the rough old work of actually trying to think things out. At any rate, the Para army padre who nicknamed me Moby would have been impressed at this moment. He had beaten the spouting and won through. I think it was then, for the first time in my life, that I understood that, God or no, there must be some control over what we are, however we got there, good or bad.

I once heard about an opera, written by a Kraut, about a man who sold his soul to the devil for a night in bed with a farm girl. He must have been daft, and certainly had never sailed the Atlantic, but I would have swopped my empty pay packet for a bird that night, bugger the devil. I went on a frantic hunt for the girlie magazine which had been thrown aboard in St John's, full of thoughts that would have earned me three hours' scrubbing floors at Fegans. I found it, a soggy mass of pulp in the bilge under the aft stowage area. It was like a bad night out in Hereford. I threw it over the side, gratefully opened my fourth can of beer kindly donated by Whitbread, cleared my mind of non-positive thoughts, read the education officer's letter again and went to bed feeling stronger and in a better state of mind than I had been in since leaving Newfoundland.

Apart from emergency inspections of the underside of the boat, I had established, in my mind at any rate, a routine set of tasks that I tried to complete on a week-to-week basis. Rudder checks meant straddling myself over the aft deck covering like a back-to-front horseman. I usually took my food from the aft end of the boat, pure laziness, I suppose, so food had to be moved from front to back at regular intervals to retrim the boat. All boring jobs, but all part of survival. Those men in St John's, with years of experience in dories, had made absolutely certain that I appreciated the importance of trim. It was the secret of the seaworthiness of that type of hull, tested over hundreds of years.

The sun appeared occasionally, but the beginning of the second week in June, almost four weeks out of Newfoundland, brought a fantastic day. Time to attack my feet again; they had been bothering me, but I had been inclined to ignore them. Now it was impossible to pretend any longer. They were bad. Sore, numb, a mass of swollen cracked skin, with toenails buried in dead white lumps hardly recognizable as toes. Sun was the first cure, so off came the plastic bags, the seaboots and socks. The apologies for feet were stuck out into the sun and fresh air. An hour later they felt better, helped by a drying with a towel and toilet paper, massage and a good dose of sun. They weren't going to drop off, but there was going to be hell to pay getting the boots back on again. There was, so I abandoned wearing boots, making do with three pairs of dry socks with plastic liners over the top until the swelling went down.

The sun disappeared again and a grey driving mist, low skies and occasional rain filled in from the west. I replenished the fresh water with rain from the covers, a bit salty and brackish, but drinkable. For five whole days I plodded on in a mental haze, rowing, eating occasionally, sleeping in a damp huddle. To be quite honest, looking back at that time, even immediately after the trip, that period, with others like it, was almost a blank. Comments in the log about wind and weather were spasmodic. It was simply survival and a desire to get eastwards, nothing else.

I shook out of it as the first month at sea ended and the dawn broke with a bright sun rising over the eastern horizon. I knew how to work out longitude by taking a dawn sunrise sight, allowing for the time difference with Greenwich (roughly) and working out the allowance. I did it and found that, assuming I was south of the latitude of Greenwich, say about 48° north, I was 48° west, 840 miles east of St John's, but I estimated, with the initial pull southeast from my departure point, I had actually covered about 1100 miles across the water to be where I was then. The Gulf Stream must be helping.

My first and only lost oar disappeared at night shortly after that. It was pure carelessness, and that angered me. It was dark and, forgetting to secure them, I shipped the oars to have a break and a brew-up. A wave hit the port side of the boat while I was on the other side. It wobbled the boat and the starboard oar shot into the darkness. I had five left, but I could not afford to lose them. I had allowed for wear and breakages, but not for that.

The next storm, my fifth, was not far away. It began at night, the worst time because one already feels more vulnerable. It was the worst so far, with winds that I estimated to be blowing at up to 70 knots. The sea was being flattened by the wind, but the occasional breaking coamer roared by. Spray stung my eyes, face and hands as I pumped water continuously. It lasted about twelve hours, leaving me in an exhausted sodden heap in the bottom of the boat. The swell was too big for rowing, so I took a tot of rum and curled up to sleep for an hour or so. The boat was taking it, but was I?

I was by now in as low a physical state as I had ever been in my life. I was fine mentally however, but a little slow in my reactions. An example of this was the moment when the cooker nearly killed me. I was making a brew of tea. I turned on the gas and then dropped the matches. As I fumbled around to find them the gas kept hissing. I struck a match and nearly blew my head off. Singed face and eyebrows added to the miseries of salt sores. The accident was caused by sheer carelessness brought on by the general slowing down of my reactions.

Flying fish appeared alongside the boat, skipping the waves, surely indicating that I was in the tropically warmed waters of the Gulf Stream, although the scudding grey clouds that crossed the sky above made it hard to believe that anything to do with the tropics was less than a million miles away. Fog and mist were a constant drain on morale, but in

'Tabbing' with 60-lb backpack

Top: I was advised to row the Atlantic 'Topper Taylor' style, seen here. It is said that Topper could row comfortably all day even in gale-force winds, but in the end I stuck to more conventional methods

Above: Sir Ernest Shackleton, the Boss

Top: Before the row – seeing a Newfoundland dory and getting some advice from its owner

Above: Super Silver

Top: Home on the range – Ardintigh

Above: Guess who's upside up!

Top: Jessie and Donald Macdonald, known as Jessie and Donald Tarbert

Above: View over Loch Morar, on the way to Ardintigh

Jill, James, Ryan the Lion and me!

mid-June I managed to take another sunrise sight with my sextant, putting me 30° west, about halfway across. Six weeks for the half distance, twelve weeks for the trip, eighty-four days total. Not bad.

5 Halfway There

Halfway, yet I had no great urge to celebrate. I was coming in range of the long-distance patrols by Shackleton aircraft from Coastal Command so it was time to unpack and check my radio ready to call if I saw or heard one. It would be good to be able to let the world know I was alive and well. I tuned the set to the calling band in the hope that there might be a friendly ear within range.

'Atlantic rowboat *Super Silver* calling. This is Moby McClean. Come in, please, come in, please.' Nothing. I felt very alone, hardly able to believe that there was no ship or aircraft listening out on that channel within 200 miles, the reputed range of the set at sea level, and there was no one more at sea level than I was, mentally and physically.

I had a few books on board. One was called *Sailing to Freedom*, about a Finnish family who escaped from the Russian invasion in the last war. They crossed the Atlantic to the United States in a small sailing boat in 130 days, going the hard way, against the prevailing winds. If they could do it so could I. A hundred and thirty days! I began carefully restoring any uneaten food in case it took me that long. Like a squirrel hiding winter nuts, I packed small plastic-covered parcels in every corner of the boat.

It was foggy, a cold dawn. I had made some tea and was reading my soggy book, miles away on another boat so far as my mind was concerned. Peace, escapism. I rowed some more, read a little, made a hot meal and rowed on. In the evening, during a reading stint, a foghorn boomed out. A ship. I jumped up and stared towards the sound. I had no radar reflector rigged, no preparations for a rendezvous.

Suddenly I saw it, about 300 yards away, a great grey monster in the swirling mist. I grabbed the radar reflector and waved it futilely above my head. No one saw it on radar or in any other way. The sea anchor was out astern to steady my drift and I knew, as the ship approached, I could never get it in in time to row towards her – or even away from her if she came too close. Hopeless, McClean, hopeless! No forward planning. No bloody thinking. Flares! That was it, fire flares, but where were they? Panic. I threw packages aside, but the ship was already past and vanishing slowly, still hooting, into the mist. Gone. I was as low as I had ever been, probably from the sudden thought of company being destroyed as fast as it had appeared. I found my box of flares, ready for the next time, sat in the bottom of the boat, arms wrapped round my knees, head buried on my arms.

At that moment of gloom I heard the hooter again. She was coming back. Perhaps someone had seen me or noticed a tiny speck on the radar. People were lining the rails waving and shouting as the ship edged towards me. I waved back.

'What do you want? What do you want?' a figure called from the bridge rail.

'My position please, just my position.'

A few moments later the same person emerged.

'You are 49 degrees 45 minutes north, 36 degrees 05 minutes west.' My own calculation, a week earlier, had been badly out. I was still about 360 miles short of halfway, but there was nothing to be done about that. The ship steamed slowly off, the crew shouting 'Good luck' in English and German. She was the *Regina Oldendorff*, from West Germany, a welcome friend indeed when needed.

I poured a tot of rum, curled up in my sleeping bag and slept for a full twelve hours, right through till morning. Then I had a cold breakfast, tea and settled down to a hard day's rowing, counting the strokes. I reached 23,000 before giving up the count. That made it about one stroke, in . . . out . . . in . . . out, every two seconds. After twelve hours nonstop, except for a lunch break, I was exhausted. Normally my day was divided into periods of rowing and other essential activities around the boat, but that day was an exception. A routine was important to fight off lethargy. I lost all sense of time in the way we know it ashore. Dawn, day, night, sleep. Hours meant little, minutes nothing at all. Days mattered, because I had worked out that after meeting the *Regina Oldendorff* I still had enough food left for another hundred days. Medical stores were in good shape, though I was low on vaseline and lanolin cream which I had been rubbing into the various sores that were still troubling me. My feet seemed better for being out of the boots.

The boat itself was in good shape, though some of the fittings, particularly the moving parts such as the rowlocks, were wearing. They creaked as I rowed, an aggravation adding to the others going through my brain. Having no engine aboard I had no oil – or had I? The answer had been there all the time. One of my favourite foods supplementing the army rations was tinned sardines in oil. Oil. Now every time I enjoyed a tin of the little fish, I drained some of the oil over the rudder pins and the rowlocks. It worked. I even felt a slight sense of achievement as the monotonous squeaking stopped. Out in the ocean, surrounded by nothingness, even the smallest success sometimes felt like climbing Everest.

One night, when sitting in the bottom of the boat thinking faraway thoughts and watching the skyline rise and dip in the waves, I saw lights far off on the horizon to the east. People. It was human contact that I was now really beginning to miss. It is something that we all take too much for granted until it's not there. There was only one answer to those feelings. I sat up on the thwart, my back towards the ship, and for a full fifteen minutes, timed on the luminous dial of my diver's watch, I rowed. I never looked over my shoulder, but when eventually I did the ship had gone.

On Sunday, 29 June, my need for company was solved, right there in the boat. My Sunday letter was from my old regimental sergeant major. His address, given at the top of the page, was: 'From where you are trying to get to . . . and will!' He told me not to worry about talking to the boat, it was all part of the game. He also told me to try talking aloud to

God, just as if he was sitting in the boat with me. I tried it and it worked. Perhaps he really was there, sitting alongside me enjoying the ride.

Next day I almost gave up. I wrote in the log that I was beginning to feel really worn down. My radio, on which I would listen to news broadcasts, had given up the struggle. Damp, I supposed. I tried new batteries, twiddling the knobs for ages. It had crackled and died, never to go again. This was another setback that seemed totally out of proportion in the middle of the ocean, just one more kick in the teeth.

The real saving factor in those low days was that there was simply no way I could give up. One could not stop a bus and hop on. Ships had been few and far enough between, so I slogged on. My sores were causing more trouble now and I had two nasty boils on my neck. I increased the daily dose of vitamin pills, four now instead of two. I felt physically dirty, the waist elastic of my oilskin trousers had perished and they fell down every time I stood up. Everything was caked with a thin rime of salt, a dust on every part of me, my kit and the boat.

The winds were helping me eastwards and I rowed mechanically for two, maybe three, days. Then, more than a week after the German meeting, I took a fix. Two, in fact, and they both came out about the same. I was inside the halfway mark at 28° 43′ west.

Again, no party, no celebration, but a renewed determination to make it to the European coast. But the wind went into the east so it was back to the sea anchor to hold me against the drift back to Canada. Then I met my first shark.

I wondered whether sharks, like vultures, sense death in the offing. However, its appearance alongside the boat gave me something to take my mind off the distance still ahead, my own physical troubles and loneliness. I think I would rather have been lonely again than have that great monster swimming with me, staring up out of the sea with evil pig-like eyes. He arrived, just after I had finished my meal, on the afternoon of 2 July, a great grey shape, complete with fin and mean long jaw. I was just putting the old tea leaves overboard when he came up, so close I could have touched him.

My God, I thought, he looks bloody ominous! He was about 15 feet long and was still there an hour later. I tried tempting him to choke to death by swallowing old empty tins, but he would have none of it. I thought of making a hook and catching him, or even sharpening the end of an oar with my bowie knife and stabbing him to death like a scene from *Moby Dick*. Scenes from films I had seen flashed through my mind. The hero, grabbing a knife and saving the damsel in distress by leaping into the sea and wrestling with the shark, or Lex Barker, whom I remembered seeing fight an alligator. No, that would simply result in *Silver* being found drifting in the ocean with no one at home.

He stayed for seven hours during the first visit, not touching the boat but eyeing it as if he knew that one good shove could have it over and a 5 foot 6½ inch meal served up for the asking. I named him Bluey and talked to him as if he were a long-lost friend. I had a pee in the bucket and threw that overboard, but it made no difference. He stayed till dusk and then suddenly flipped over and vanished.

'Get lost!' I called out at him, 'and don't come back,' but he did, next day, again after lunch. Again he stayed for ages, circling the boat, occasionally disappearing only to bob up on the other side. To reassure myself, or to take my mind off the problem, I tried the radio again, but without success; they were either too far away or not listening, whoever might have answered. Bluey shot off west when dusk fell, and I slept fitfully, imagining him swimming just below the hull, separated from me by only a thin layer of wood. Next day the wind went into the east and while it headed me it seemed to have given Bluey other thoughts. He set off to the west.

Then my airbed burst, the result of constant chafing and continual soaking in gritty salt. I tried mending it with plastic tape, Bostik and Elastoplast, but nothing worked and I had forgotten to bring a puncture repair kit with me. One cannot remember or foresee everything.

I slept well that night, in spite of having less between my sore bruised body and the deck, but next morning I awoke depressed. I also had the shakes, there is no other way of describing the trouble. My legs and knees shook uncontrollably. It was almost like vertigo when a climber freezes on a rock face, except that I was in the bottom of the boat almost unable to stand properly. I tried massage, found that I could stand more easily and set about pulling myself together yet again. A good curry was needed, but all I really felt like eating was tinned fruit salad, and that with effort. I *had* to pull myself together – it was that or die.

The smell of the cooking curry, which normally induced pangs of hunger, made me feel totally nauseated, but I had to eat it even if it took me the rest of the day. Then the shark came back, as if he had smelled the curry and wanted some himself. I concentrated on eating, forcing each spoonful into my mouth, watching the shark. Then I realized that there were five or more fins round the boat, but the nearest, I was sure, was Bluey. I could recognize the markings on his head. I took photographs of him, almost as therapy for myself, a morale booster, but it reminded me of the matelot plaiting his own cat-o'-nine-tails before being flogged.

Despite the gloom and despondency I had been doing quite a bit of rowing. The winds were with me and I was moving east, but I could not have told anyone how long or how well I had rowed; it was completely mechanical. Thunder woke me one night, a crack right overhead that nearly blasted me out of the boat. Old army reactions came back to remind me of other times past. The storm lasted about four hours, filling the sky with light and sound while rain streaked down and a contrary wind increased, undoing all my efforts at the oars, or so I became more and more convinced as I cowered below trying to sleep a little. It was impossible to row in that storm which raged well into morning. The easterly wind continued for ages, with me rowing against it trying not to lose ground. Hopeless, but it was better than going backwards feeling sorry for myself.

The seas rose again and I had to stop rowing, but a pain in my arms woke me from the doziness. Cooking and sleeping, then the wind dropped and went west again. Hurray! Back to work.

July 9th, fifty-three days out, the westerlies really settled in for twelve wonderful days. On the same day I passed foot inspection with flying colours. They were almost as good as new. I could wear my boots again, but was determined to pay daily attention to them so they would never become as bad as they had been. Next day I heard a plane flying somewhere ahead, a sound of the land. I thought of harvest and remembered a cable from the Venns. 'Make it home for harvest.' What would I not give for the smell of a field, a wood, just the good earth? I tried a sextant sunrise fix to boost me further and found I was about 720 miles from Ireland, but with this wind my average was rising. How much longer? I didn't dare calculate it; that would be tempting fate.

Despair was fading fast, replaced by a new enthusiasm now that I knew I was going to make it. Although I would not calculate the time still to be done at sea, the number twenty-four kept going through my brain. I rowed day and night, cat-napping and eating between rowing sessions, three hours on, an hour for main meal, row, an hour for tea and a kip, row. On and on. Press on!

I had a rum at 2 a.m. and rowed onwards. I saw great pools of light in the sea where a large fish, maybe a whale, was disturbing the water as it rose from the deep. I saw ships occasionally, far off, just like lights on a small Christmas tree. On, onward . . . at three miles an hour, that was the target, plus help from wind and current.

On 13 July I saw a ship far away. I thought it might be the weather ship *Juliet* which I knew worked in this area. I fired a flare. No good. Then I fired a radar flare which at 2000 feet burst into a mass of metal particles which would make a big blob on a radar screen. It nearly blew me out of the boat as it went off and left my face black with soot, but it worked and the ship turned towards me.

She was the *Hansa*, out of Deptford, bound for London with newsprint for the Express group – my story no doubt. When she was close to me, the captain left the bridge and came to the midship deck. The conversation was the same as before: food, drink, even a bath was offered, but, heart in mouth, I had to decline. He gave me my position, took several rolls of film from me and a note, promising to report my position to Lloyds and Express Newspapers. Then, giving me time to row clear of the screws, he was off to the east.

Once he had gone I checked my position. I was only 10°, a mere 600 miles, from Ireland. Rum, a small celebration, and back to rowing. But the Atlantic had not done with me yet.

I was in such good form now that during the next three or four days I began singing as I rowed, old favourites like 'Danny Boy' and 'Over the Sea to Skye'. I have a terrible voice, but who cared out there? My elation was short-lived. Five days after seeing the *Hansa*, I was sleeping under the cover at about 2.30 a.m. The sea had grown too rough to allow me to row, so I decided to rest, ready to start when the swell moderated. Suddenly I was awake, feeling as if I were inside a spin drier, my clothes, food, equipment and other stores whirling round with me. The whole boat filled with water. It had been rolled over, probably twice or three times, but had been saved from complete disaster by the dodger canvases pulled over the cockpit. They held everything in the boat and prevented a sudden total swamping. *Silver* finally settled the right way up and I fought my way past the life raft which was jammed against the dodger, but even though I was standing in the boat I was waist deep in water. Both ends of the hull were above water, but the entire cockpit area was filled to the gunwales. Only those polystyrene buoyancy spaces were keeping us on the surface. I found the bucket tied in its right place, but how do you bale out a boat that is floating under water? I thought quickly and as I moved I noticed that the rocking motion brought each gunwale in turn to the surface, a little more each time. I started rocking.

The water cleared slowly until there was about six inches freeboard on each side. It took, it seemed, an age, but probably no more than three minutes. The storm had eased and dawn was breaking as I started on the pump and baled for all I was worth. Two weeks earlier I doubt I would have coped, but the old spirits were up to drive me on. What had caused the capsize, that was the question I had to ask. The sea had been rough, but *Silver* and I had survived worse. Then I saw the sea anchor. One of the lines to which it had been attached was broken at the swivel. It seemed that with the sea anchor off to one side of the boat, *Silver* had swung across the waves and been rolled by a larger one than the others, perhaps my weight on the side away from the wind and waves helping in the process. Once over and filled with water the boat was like a rubber ball, the same weight as the sea, weightless in fact, and unstable.

I was in a state of virtual collapse once the boat was dry, trembling with a combination of shock, effort, fear and tiredness. It was to be sleep first and then a sortout of the boat. Sleep came slowly, but when it did it was deep. I woke that evening, ate some cold rations and a tin of fruit and set about drying the stove and finding myself new dry clothes from the plastic bundles under the aft deck. Then more sleep, following some liquid intake. Amazingly, very few things had been lost in the capsize, but the chaos was a marvel to see. I was soon asleep, but up with the early dawn to start sorting out the confusion. I felt great again. Breakfast was a real feast: hot porridge with honey on top, two Mars bars, marmalade on biscuits, all washed down with coffee laced with rum.

It was a day-long job, checking for damage inside and outside the boat, sorting stores, drying bits and pieces. Two gallons of fresh water seemed to have gone and all my charts except that of the whole North Atlantic and the coast of Ireland.

Sunday, 20 July, was letter-opening day, one from the quartermaster back at Hereford. He told me to stick at it. Well, there was little alternative. Under leaden skies I started rowing against southeasterly winds, winds heading me north.

Trim was vital now, with half the food gone and the stores depleted, so I intentionally flooded various compartments in the bottom of the boat. The wind freshened and veered to the west, helping me along. I even managed to take a fix in the dawn, putting me only 240 miles from land. Two hundred and forty miles, a mere tenth of the total distance to be covered. I was nearly there, having been at sea for sixty-five days. I was not really confident that I knew where I was, so I started looking out for signs of land: shore-based seabirds, seaweed, anything to give me a clue that I had not been swept too far north. My first clue was not one that I was watching out for. An airliner passed overhead, heading west and still climbing to the altitude that produced the contrails that I had seen on the way across. Could this aircraft be climbing out from Shannon Airport, on the Irish west coast? I hoped so. New energy went into my rowing. I don't think I had rowed as well the whole way across from Newfoundland. I only stopped for meal breaks on my sixty-eighth day, finally stopping at 10 p.m. for a meal and a good dreamless sleep that lasted until the cold dawn woke me.

Next day, to my frustration, the wind backed to the southeast but two coastal fishing boats appeared two miles ahead. I thought of sending up a flare, but decided against it, but it was a warning. I must be about four days off, so the kit had to be prepared for a landing on a rough rocky shore. Hand flares, logbook, films, rations, medical kit, cameras, all these went into a special plastic container bound with tape. I rowed throughout Friday, the 25th, late into the evening. Then, after the now customary tot of rum, I slept fitfully as if someone was chipping at my mind. At dawn I woke, looked around and started to brew a cup of coffee. I drank it slowly still looking about me, and began to row once more.

I had an anorak tied to my telescopic radio aerial but it was not sighted by the ship that I saw off to my starboard side. I made some tea and sat sipping it as I looked around. I thought I saw a shadow on the horizon to the east, stared long at it, but it faded. Cloud, or smoke from a ship? Never mind, I must not dream. I must row. At 10.30 I was off again and an hour later I looked over my shoulder. There was no doubt this time, *land*. The first I had seen for over two months. *Land! Land!* I jumped around the boat cheering out loud. I was nearly there, about eight hours from the shore, but in eight hours it would be getting dark. As I rowed steadily onwards, southeast now, towards that smudge on the edge of the sea, I thought carefully. I was fairly sure, after looking carefully at my Irish coast chart, that I was approaching the Mullet peninsula, on the County Mayo coast of Eire.

That afternoon a fishing boat, the *Ebba Victor*, closed with me.

'Are you all right?' called the skipper.

'Am I!' I called. 'I have never felt better. Never! Is that Mullet?'

'It is,' came back the Irish voice and with no more ado they steamed off. It was a bit of a letdown, but what should I have expected?

Later that afternoon I stopped to re-examine my position. It was taking longer than I expected to get close to the shore. The wind was going into the south, pushing me out, and night was still five hours away. I battled on towards the headland where I could just see breaking water at the foot of the cliffs. I wanted to round the headland and find what I was sure would be shelter on the other side, but I needed to be closer to make sure. The wind was stronger and I knew that I would not get in that night.

It was a disappointment, but the right decision not to try, even if it had been possible. I rowed all night and at 2 a.m. on Sunday I could clearly see the flash of a lighthouse. As dawn began to throw the first fingers of light into the eastern sky I could see rocks below the light and the entrance of a large bay. I aimed for it, putting everything I had left in me into the rowing. My landing pack was near my feet, tied to me by a line, and for the first time I was wearing my lifejacket, uninflated at the moment. The sound of breaking surf grew louder and at 5.30 a.m. we struck rocks, large slabs of stone, not the jagged teeth-like spikes that I had dreaded. I jumped, hitting my knee hard as I landed, and scrambled for dry land, the sea dumping me unceremoniously on the ledge above the boat, which was being pounded on the rocks below me by the wind-powered swell.

As I watched the boat being thumped about, I knew I had to save her after all we had been through. I could not leave *Silver* to become a heap of mangled plywood. I jumped back down the rock face and put my shoulder to the bow. It took me a quarter of an hour to swing the bow out towards the waves, but I did it and, banged and bruised, clambered back aboard as a receding wave carried us out to sea once more. I unshipped the oars and for another hour fought my way out to sea past the spit on which the lighthouse stood. Several times the oars struck rocks, but after a further hour the water became suddenly calm as we rounded the headland. In front of us was a beautiful sheltered bay with hundreds of yards of smooth sandy beach stretching away on either side.

I rowed steadily towards it, my body finding a new energy,

and struck the beach with a healthy thud just after 7.30 a.m. on Sunday, 27 July 1969. I heaved *Silver* as far up the beach as I could and then tied the bow line to a large boulder. There was not a soul in sight. The boat looked a bit of a mess, so I found a brush and scrubbed some of the weed off her, tidied the end lockers and cockpit and folded the covers as neatly as I could. There was no more to be done, so I picked up the landing pack and headed up the beach.

Just over the back of the beach I found a small cottage. An old lady stood at the door watching me. I must have been quite a sight with my straggly beard and salt-stained clothes. I shouted out to her.

'Good morning. I've just rowed the Atlantic. Can I take your photograph?' She looked nervous, obviously thinking that a madman was after her, but before she edged back through her door and firmly closed it, I asked her where I was and just caught her reply as she vanished into the house. Blacksod Bay. Not exactly a hero's welcome, but they were the sweetest words I had heard for ten weeks. I slung my pack on my shoulder and strode on up the unmade road, and there, just a quarter of a mile away, was the only pub in the tiny village on that wild piece of the west Irish Coast. Being Ireland, the welcome was as only the Irish know how.

6 A Hunt for a Home

After it was all over I went back to the army in Hereford. Before I had set out I had left £100 with the NAAFI manager, to be spent on beer if I did not make it back. I found that my friends had already drunk it, celebrating my return while I was still at sea.

I seemed to have become quite famous. I was made a freeman of the City of Hereford at a welcome-home ceremony attended by most of the members of the SAS stationed at Hereford at the time. I was also asked to give lectures at Rotary Clubs, but this was not really my idea of fun.

In January 1970 *Silver* went to the Boat Show at Earl's Court in London, where I manned the stand for ten long days, signing autographs, talking to people and even having to deal with a couple of chinless wonders, probably too full of Guinness from the famous Boat Show Guinness stand, who said that they did not believe that I had done the trip. One of the main questions was what I planned to do next. The more people I saw the more I wanted to escape from them. It was all part of the general pattern, the loner side of me coming out on top. I decided to leave the SAS. I had been offered all sorts of jobs in civilian life, but I headed for the Venns at the farm to give myself time to think out what I really wanted to do.

I drove for miles in my Mini car, to north Wales, Scotland and other more remote places. North Wales seemed too crowded, but on the Isle of Mull I was able to make friends with the local people. I had been invited by Lord Maclean to stay at Duart Castle and see the island. I first met him in London when the Clan Maclean were holding a reunion. Now, with the idea of an adventure centre forming in my mind, this seemed to be a great chance to look at the possibilities. Lord Maclean was Queen's Chamberlain so I was starting among the right people.

Mull is a beautiful island, the second largest in the Inner Hebrides, and Lord Maclean asked one of his employees to show me round. I had decided to buy some land, as remote as possible, and build cabins on it so that all sorts of people could come along and use it as a base for expeditions, climbing, canoeing, or simply to get away from the rush of modern life. While I was there I met Neil and Janet Macgillivray, from Rossal Farm at Pennyghael, who are friends to this day. I also met another Maclean, who ran the Clansman Restaurant in the village of Pennyghael, on the road to Iona, the famous shrine off the southwest coast of Mull.

He offered to sell me his restaurant and worked hard to convince me that I, with my nonexistent knowledge of catering, bars and business affairs, could manage to run it. At the back of the restaurant was a field, which attracted me as a possible site. Mr Maclean persuaded me into working as a barman there to see how it went while I thought about buying the place. Back in the south, when I went down there to gather my few belongings, friends were more practical and began talking me out of the idea. It would be a millstone around my neck; I had no wife to help run the business and would be tied there 365 days a year. They suggested that I buy the field but leave the restaurant for someone else with more experience, a more settled way of life, and perhaps more sense.

During my wandering between the south and Scotland, where my hunt for a piece of land continued, one or two incidents occurred which made me realize that although I had left the armed forces I was not necessarily forgotten by those with whom I had served. On one occasion, while staying with the Venns, I received a telephone call from someone whom I did not know but who certainly knew all about me, right down to my telephone number at the farm and the length of time I was planning to be there.

The caller asked whether I was interested in doing a one-off military operation abroad which would earn me a respectable sum of money. If I was interested, after thinking it over, I was to go to London two days later and report to an address in the West End. Nothing more was said at that stage. As I needed cash for my land-buying operation, after some thought I went to the address. There were several familiar faces there from my earlier days in the Paras and the SAS, and others whom I did not know.

We were given a brief and sketchy outline of what might be involved by a man who described himself as the Leader. It was a job abroad, as the telephone caller had said; it involved weapon training and the use of military skills and would be paid for in cash banked wherever we wanted. No other details were given, but those not interested were asked to leave while the rest of us were invited to go home and think it over, reporting to the same place the following week if we wanted to take part. Everyone was given some money for attending that first meeting. Afterwards I returned to the farm.

During a week of thinking and farming I decided to go back to London. The numbers had dwindled a little. We were given no more details other than a slight elaboration on those of the previous week, but were asked to travel independently to Scotland for training and fitness exercises. What was in the wind involved boats, guns, explosives and fitness. Other than that we knew almost nothing. Money was paid regularly during our stay in Scotland and then, as quickly as the whole thing had started, it ended. Again, no reasons were given, no locations mentioned or other information passed on. We were paid off and each man made his own way home.

Later I heard of mercenary forces being involved in actions abroad, some of my old colleagues actually appearing in newspapers when one of these operations went wrong. My own brief experience of this type of life was enough to prove two things: I was still as fit as I had been in the services, and the life of a mercenary soldier was not for me. It was too insecure, covert and risky. I had had my share of that sort of thing and preferred to control my own life rather than have it controlled by secretive people who were obviously going to make more out of my skills than I was. I had left the army. It was time to stop being a soldier and start trying to make an honest go of civilian life. So, back north on my quest for land on which I could live and earn a living.

I was still making the occasional appearance at shows and clubs, and it was while on the way to a boat show in Leicester, towing *Silver* behind the car and driving much too fast, that I almost came to grief. The boat was on a trailer which I had made from a caravan chassis. The trailer was snaking a bit as we travelled up the M1. I slowed, controlled the snaking, but a lorry came up on my outside and touched the side of the trailer. It began to zigzag badly. Suddenly trailer and car began going right round, in the centre of the motorway, making at least three complete turns before the trailer wheel caught the offside verge, turned the whole thing over and the trailer rolled on top of the boat.

At first no one stopped to help; then several lorry drivers pulled in, the police arrived and we righted the whole muddle. My licence had lapsed but the police gave me a warning, realizing who I was, I expect, and told me to get on my way before they caught up again – and to get a licence. I gave them a photograph of me and the boat, which made them happy.

I worked in the bar at Pennyghael for three months but the owner began to have second thoughts about selling it. I spent some time with the Macgillivrays, eventually staying with them in their croft when the bar job and aspirations of becoming a restaurateur came to an end. I was there for two months, working, stalking in the hills and generally thinking out my next move, which was south once more, back to the Venns at the farm. My heart was still set on an adventure centre, but the question was how I was going to be able to afford the land, and the cost of building on it. It was then that I telephoned David Stirling, the founder of the SAS, and asked whether he could help or had any ideas, particularly so far as land was concerned.

His response was instant. Typical of the man. He told me that his cousin, Lord Lovat, who had formed the famous Lovat Scouts, founders of the Commando regiments, owned

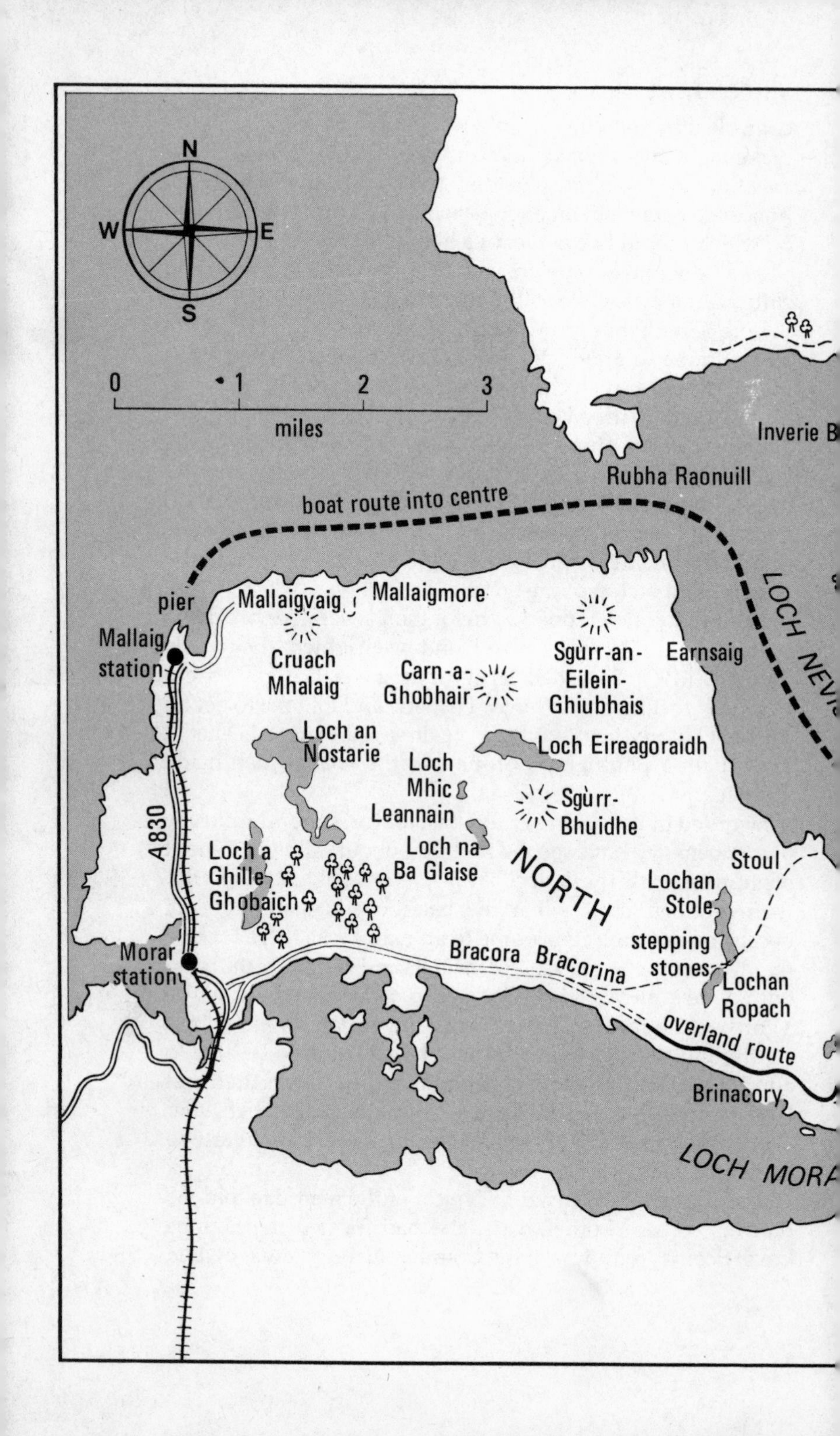
N
W
E
S
0
1
2
3
miles
Inverie B
Rubha Raonuill
boat route into centre
LOCH NEVIS
pier
Mallaigvaig
Mallaigmore
Mallaig
station
Cruach
Mhalaig
Carn-a-
Ghobhair
Sgùrr-an-
Eilein-
Ghiubhais
Earnsaig
Loch an
Nostarie
Loch Eireagoraidh
Loch
Mhic
Leannain
Sgùrr-
Bhuidhe
A830
Loch a
Ghille
Ghobaich
Loch na
Ba Glaise
NORTH
Stoul
Lochan
Stole
stepping
stones
Morar
station
Bracora
Bracorina
Lochan
Ropach
overland route
Brinacory
LOCH MORA

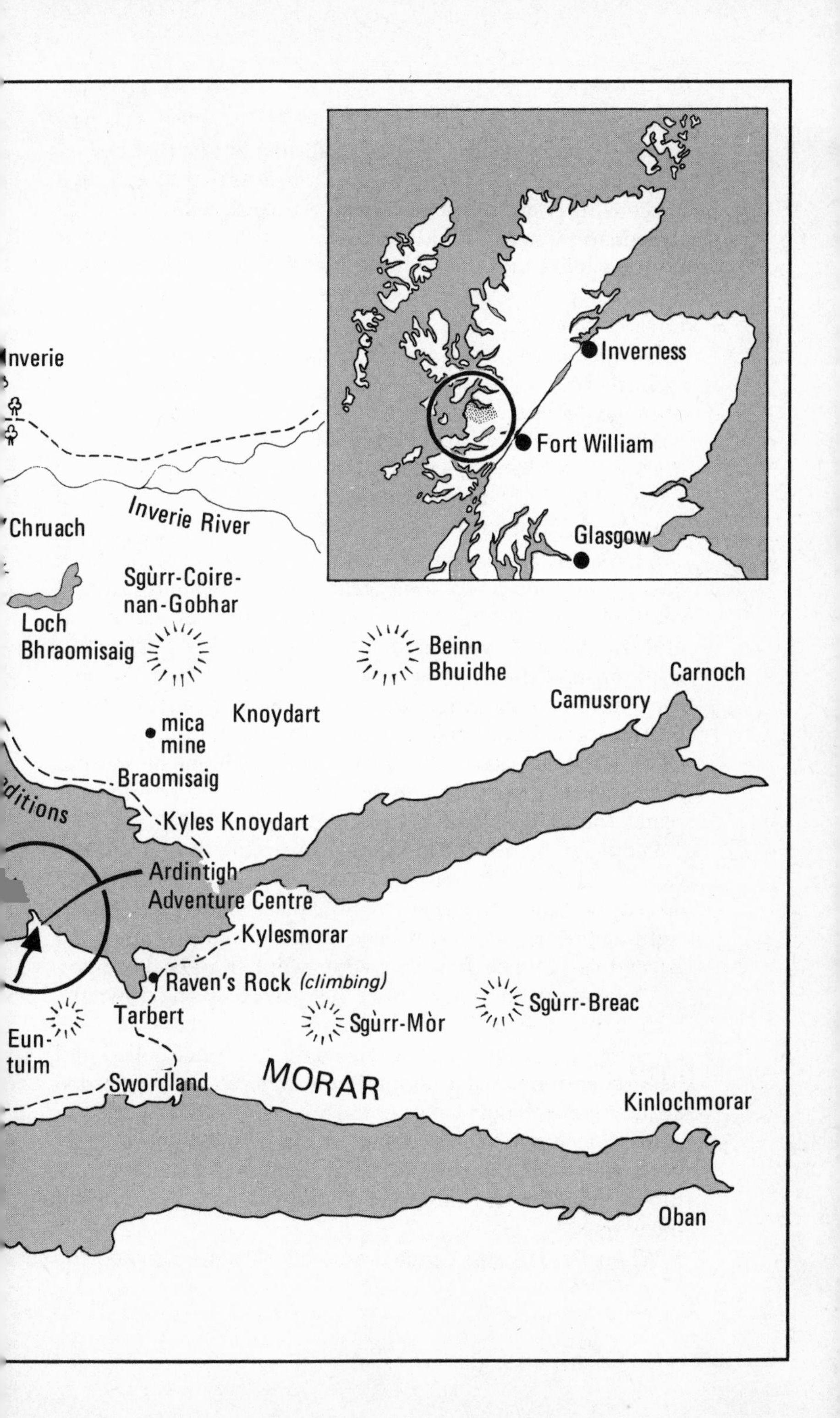
Inverness
Fort William
Glasgow
Inverie
Inverie River
Chruach
Loch
Bhraomisaig
Sgùrr-Coire-
nan-Gobhar
Beinn
Bhuidhe
Carnoch
Camusrory
Knoydart
mica
mine
Braomisaig
ditions
Kyles Knoydart
Ardintigh
Adventure Centre
Kylesmorar
Raven's Rock (climbing)
Sgùrr-Breac
Tarbert
Sgùrr-Mòr
Eun-
tuim
MORAR
Swordland
Kinlochmorar
Oban

land in western Scotland. It was from the people of this part of the country, ghillies, stalkers, hill shepherds, that he had selected the scouts. David put the phone down, then called his cousin. Thirty minutes later he was back, telling me to go to Scotland where I could stay with his sister Irenie at Morar Lodge while I looked around for land. I was off like a shot, heading up the road from Glasgow to Fort William and on towards Mallaig.

I arrived at Morar Lodge, a superb house on the shoreline of Loch Morar, south of Mallaig on the peninsula. Irenie Stirling was a perfect and helpful hostess. She suggested that I went across the water to Knoydart where the local Mallaig doctor, Donald Duck, was staying on holiday. Apparently he knew all the local landowners and would have some idea of what land might be available.

I took the local ferry from Mallaig to Inverie, on Loch Nevis, and then had a long walk, about eight miles, until I reached Airor, on the coast overlooking the Sound of Sleat and the Isle of Skye. The doctor was staying a further five miles around the coast, so I borrowed a boat from a namesake, another Maclean, and made the trip in about one and a half hours with the small Seagull outboard manfully shoving away. When I reached the doctor's holiday home he was out fishing. I met his wife and children and we discussed my plans, the children being most enthusiastic.

People in that part of the world are careful, thoughtful and canny – their word that sums it all up. There had been an adventure school at a really remote place called Camusrory, right at the head of Loch Nevis, run for children from Dr Barnado's Homes. It was a windswept, rain-beaten spot, catching every piece of weather that passed up and down the loch, hardly the ideal place for a bunch of town children used to parks, pavements and a few comforts. It had failed and been abandoned. The locals knew this, so were guarded against another newcomer to the area who probably did not appreciate just how bad things could be up there. It must have been more like combat survival training than an adventure holiday for the children when the weather took a turn for the worse.

When Dr Barnado's pulled out, the staff approached the

local landowners and formed the Travellers Trust, money being provided by the local estates, but eventually, after several years, it failed again. The doctor and his wife put it to me that if an organization like the Travellers Trust, with local financial backing, could not make a go of it, how would I expect to, on my own, living out in the hills on the edge of the loch? I told them that I would build a small hut, fish for lobsters from a boat, and gradually build up from there. They were not rude, but fairly adamant that I was on a hiding to nothing. However, the children said that if my scheme worked, it would be great fun.

This made me more determined than ever. I thanked them for their advice and left, my brain humming with ideas. I was going to do it, if only to prove them wrong. It was the sort of ambition that had helped so many times in the past.

It was the old story. If someone says that something cannot be done, then my attitude was, and still is, to turn round and have a damned good try. I went back to Morar Lodge and told Irenie what had happened. She was not discouraging but suggested that next day I should walk over the hill to Loch Nevis and meet Donald and Jessie Macdonald who lived on Loch Nevis at Tarbert. They ran the loneliest post office in Britain. A rough track led there and it was only really accessible by water from Mallaig, a distance of nine miles up the loch. For me, it was a walk of two hours along the side of Loch Morar, a long inland loch with its own monster, Morag, and then through a gap in the hills to Loch Nevis. It was an exhilarating walk and Donald and Jessie, typical crofters, were happy to see me and talk over tea and homemade cake.

They suggested that I look at a derelict place called Ardintigh, about two miles down the loch towards Mallaig. They told me that there was the remains of a field, a broken-down croft with a tree growing in it and a small stone beach. Donald said that if it was what I wanted, he, as crofter of the land, would sell the rights back to the estate and they could then rent it to me. It all seemed too easy. Donald and I walked over the steep shoulder to have a look at it. I had my tent and a few stores with me, so stayed there for a few days looking about. Then I went back to see Donald to tell him I was going to have a try at making something of the place. A quiet man of great inner strength and deep religious convictions, he seemed pleased, wished me luck, and I headed off back to Morar to give Irenie the news.

7 Ardintigh

It was December. I wanted to be with the Venns for Christmas and New Year, but could not wait to get cracking on my patch of land. My first stay there had been interesting and my SAS training had stood me in good stead. That first dark evening, I had pitched my small tent, made a fire, and cooked my first of many meals at Ardintigh. I had listened to the wind humming across the loch, seen the faint moon lighting the distant snow-covered peaks and watched a sea otter hunting for his supper in the shallows off the small headland to the east of the abandoned field, now a mass of dead bracken. After more than six months, nearer nine, of hunting for a place, I had found it. Home. It felt strangely welcoming, as if it needed someone to be there to bring life back to what had once been a small community, whittled down in numbers by wars and the general drift of young people to the towns and bright lights. I had slept the sleep of a happy man, covered with a poncho cape, curled up in my sleeping bag on a bed of bracken which I had dried as best I could by the fire.

Irenie was to put the wheels in motion with the estate while I went to collect my few possessions and see the Venns. She was infected by my excitement and, although the houses up there were few and far apart, it was not long before news got round that a small mad Irishman had camped for a couple of days in mid-December out at Ardintigh. At least he had a Scottish name. They were already quietly interested and

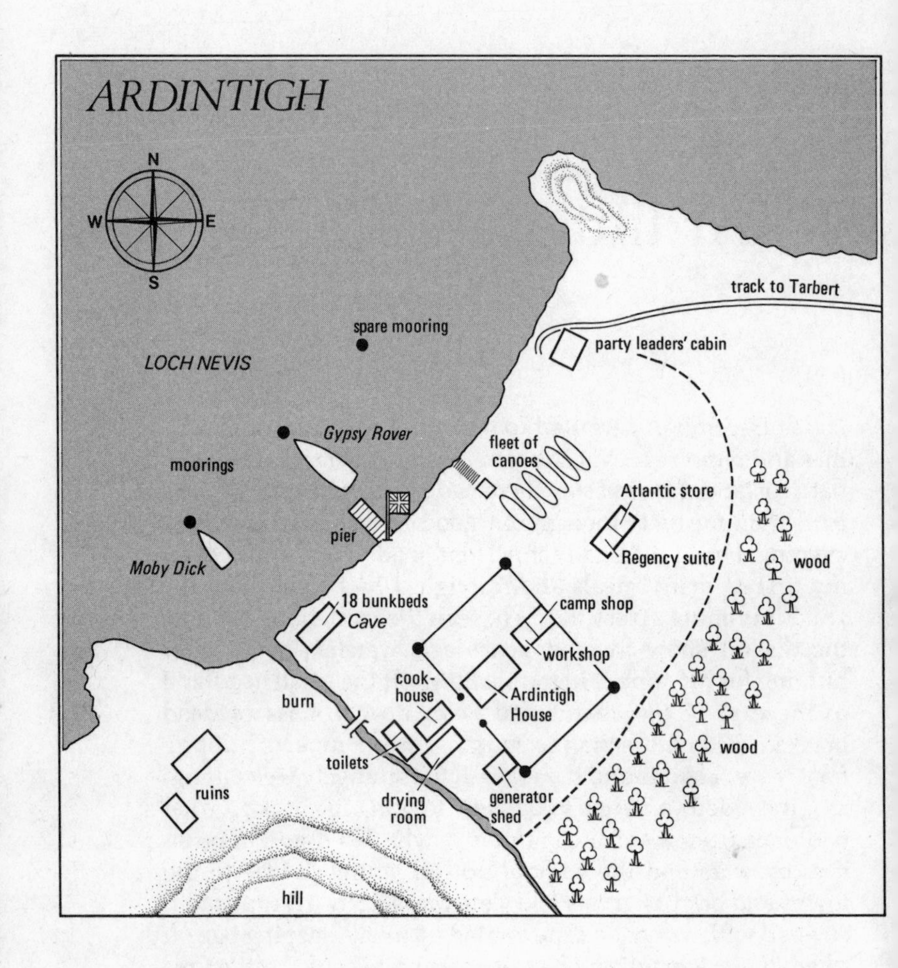
ARDINTIGH
N
W
E
S
track to Tarbert
spare mooring
party leaders' cabin
LOCH NEVIS
Gypsy Rover
fleet of canoes
moorings
Atlantic store
pier
Regency suite
wood
Moby Dick
18 bunkbeds
Cave
camp shop
workshop
cook-house
Ardintigh House
burn
wood
toilets
ruins
drying room
generator shed
hill

watching when I returned in the van in the new year of 1971.

I arrived at Morar and found digs in the village with Angie MacLellan who lived in a house called Curtaig. I wanted to get out to Ardintigh as soon as possible but needed a boat. That was the first priority as it was the only way to reach the place in winter. I stayed with Angie for almost two weeks while I searched for a suitable boat. I found one, belonging to Ian MacEachan, of Arisaig, an 18-foot conventional clinker-built boat, good and solid. I paid him £200 and then went off to look for an outboard engine.

The papers granting me rights to use the land had been drawn up by the Lovat Estate. I was ready to go to my own patch. I loaded all my belongings into the boat, watched, as always, by the local people, who were obviously filled with curiosity. They said little, were polite and helpful, but I could tell that they thought I was not far from mad. Some wished me luck. I headed out of Mallaig harbour, round the point to the northeast and up the long narrow loch. The wind-whipped water splashed into my face as I made my way across the grey expanse, looking for my headland. Two hours later, well soaked, I saw it and half an hour after that I inched in to the boulder-strewn beach. It seemed bleaker than when I had camped there a few weeks earlier, with the wind whistling through the tree growing out of the remains of the croft and the steep hill rising up behind the apology of a field.

I jumped out of the boat into the cold water and took the bow rope up the beach to a boulder, tying it as best I could. I had to work fast to unload the boat as a squall was threatening. The light was fading and darkness approaching even though it was only mid-afternoon.

I beached the boat once it was unloaded, pulling it a little farther up the beach as it became lighter. Then I pitched my tent, an igloo type with inflatable arms at each corner. I decided to put it in the ruins of the croft for shelter but the floor was damp so I built it up with stones and put the tent on top of this, supported by guy ropes at each corner. I lit a fire outside and found an oil lamp in my pile of stores. There was no other light in sight, yet I could see thirty miles in one direction, to the mountains of Skye, and about seven in the other. I cooked a meal from tins, unpacked my sleeping bag and went to bed, exhausted but happy. It was the end of January 1971.

The last person to live at Ardintigh had been Peggy Macdonald, known locally as Peggy Ardintigh. She had lost her son in the First World War and had gone to Mallaig where she used to wander round the small port telling all who cared to listen that God had forgotten her. She died in Mallaig and the croft that had been her home had fallen to the ground. Now, as a tenant, I was lord of all I surveyed and at a very unlordly rent of £15 per year.

For the first few days I wandered around planning. I would walk over to Donald's and Jessie's for a cup of tea and more planning, making lists of things that I had to buy in Mallaig. My first job was to build a septic tank big enough to cope with the camp I was going to build, which would, I hoped, eventually house up to twenty-four people.

I took the boat to Mallaig and bought crowbars, axes, sledge-hammers and cold chisels. Then I went back to Ardintigh and, near the water's edge, in the best possible site, began to dig a hole 8 feet square and, so I intended, 9 feet deep. I started digging. At about 4 feet down I hit hard rock. While I was digging or resting from this backbreaking work, I had seen a small speedboat a couple of times rushing up the loch towards Donald's place at Tarbert. At the end of the second week it came towards my beach and out stepped a priest, Father Murphy, a wonderful and amusing Irishman. Once every two weeks in those days he went to the little church, now closed, at Tarbert, and said mass with Donald and Jessie, just the three of them. He had come across the loch from Inverie. We started to chat and I brewed some tea. He took a cup, walked down the beach, inspected the hole and turned to me.

'Come on, Tom, I'm not too busy, give me a pick and shovel. I'll give you a break.'

I made another brew and sat back to watch. There was only room for one person in the hole, so it was a welcome rest. He worked for five hours almost without a stop, had another brew of tea and then was on his way, giving a cheery wave as he went. We became great friends from that day. He would often call in at Ardintigh on his way from island to island visiting the strong Catholic community which lives on the western coast of Scotland and the small isles, as they are known.

I finished digging the hole, but when I had rendered it, water kept seeping up through the rock. It ran down off the hill behind the camp over the layer of hard rock. It took me a week or two to cure it, rendering the hole with dry cement, and in the end I won.

After I had finished the tank, I heard from a friend from Aylesbury. Steve Mitchell, or Mitch as I called him, had been out of school a year or two and wanted to come to Scotland to lend a hand. He wrote to me via the post office at Mallaig. I explained that there would be no money in the job but that he was welcome. Any help was! He arrived, delighted to get away from life in the south for a while.

The next stage was to build some permanent huts. The obvious type was prefabricated timber cabins. I contacted the firm of Blacks, at Forres, beyond Inverness, which manufactured just what I needed. Unfortunately my boat, now named *Moby Dick*, was not big enough to carry the sections, some as long as 20 feet. My friend Ian MacEachan, at Arisaig, who had sold me the boat, said that he would rent me his own boat for the job, a double-ended whaler with a pine deck. The cabin floors were the most awkward and heaviest components. We put a railway sleeper across the boat and laid the sections on this. The boat rode low in the water carrying a complete hut in pieces. I was perched out at the stern on a timber extension. In this manner I made my way slowly and carefully back to Ardintigh.

Four or five local people, who had by now become friends and realized I meant business, offered to come up to Ardintigh in another boat and help Mitch and me unload the cabins. Among them were George Lawrie and his brother Archie; they were well known for their famous Mallaig kippers. It was cold work, everyone having to wade out waist deep into the loch to lift the sections off the boat. It took all day, and we made four trips back to Mallaig to collect each of the huts. By evening, cold and tired, not to mention wet, we had four huts in pieces on the foreshore. It was very satisfying. Things were moving ahead. I had only been at Ardintigh for two months, still living in the tent, but with the septic tank, the promise of huts, and ready for the next stage – laying foundations and drains.

I had already begun clearing the bracken that covered the field, scything the new shoots as they appeared, having burnt and raked off the dead plants from the previous year. It took three years to kill it off completely, but grass lay below. Once the bracken was cut down, the place began to look quite smart. Now I needed help to erect the huts, so I contacted Bernie Franks who had been at Hereford, attached to the SAS as a carpenter when I was building and modifying *Super Silver*. He was now with the 33rd Squadron, Royal Engineers, serving in Northern Ireland. I asked him if he would like to bring some soldiers over for a 'rest and recuperation' to put up the huts. I already had the footings in place. He accepted and came with the first squad of soldiers to visit the camp. They finished the job, doing some canoeing and walking between working. We all had a good time and everyone enjoyed themselves, even if the place was still very basic. It was to set the pattern for the years ahead. The soldiers' enthusiasm gave me the beginnings of an idea. Four huts were up, spring was in the air and it was time to think about fishing. I had decided to buy thirty or forty lobster pots, creels as they are called in Scotland, and pay my way by fishing. I had been living on soups, the occasional curry, and bread and jam until then and needed some cash. A Mallaig fisherman was selling his old creels at a low price, and there were fifty of them, so I bought the lot. I started fishing close inshore with one pot per line and float. (The locals fished with twenty pots per line.) Mitch and I used to set our pots, one at a time, and then go back to work at the camp while the lobsters got themselves caught. We caught about ten a day, good going by anyone's reckoning and enough to keep us in funds and food, although we seldom ate lobster ourselves; it was a luxury food, money, not for us.

As the evenings lengthened we would go north across the loch to Inverie, to a club run for the estate people, where we would have a dram or a few beers and meet the locals. There were no pubs for miles, the ones in Mallaig being the nearest (and that is still the case).

By now not only was word getting to various army units about the camp as a potential adventure centre, but units were arriving to help me put it together. They came in small groups and camped rough in the huts, cooking for themselves on open fires and living a very rugged, open-air life. Between doing the various jobs, they climbed the hills roundabout, swam and explored the wild countryside near the camp. This was fine in high summer, but in spring and autumn, when the frosts were quite severe, there was need for more permanent accommodation.

One or two people might get the impression that I was using the army to feather my nest, but this was not the case. I paid for all the materials for building the camp; they provided the muscle. Once the word went round from unit to unit, I could not keep them away. As I write this, ten years after those early days, we have just said goodbye to units of my old battalion, 3 Para, at Ardintigh for rest and recuperation. They pay me a modest amount of money for the facilities while they do their own catering, plan their own routine and look after themselves.

Another point that must be emphasized is that the camp is not, never has been, a training centre for military activities. There are no weapons at the camp except my own licensed hunting rifle. All the activities are leisure oriented, even if, at times, tough. Some units will try everything – climbing, abseilling, canoeing, anything the countryside can offer. Others will do very little – a few walks, swimming and drinking many cans of beer, enjoying a real holiday. The decision as to what they do at Ardintigh has always rested with themselves, their instructors or the officers in charge.

Anyway, back to that spring of 1971. The next task was to organize an electricity supply and build a toilet block. I read in *Exchange and Mart* that there was a Lister two and a half kilowatt single-cylinder diesel generator for sale near Inverness. One of the officers with the soldiers staying at the time had a big American Dodge with a trailer, so I asked him if in exchange for the cost of the petrol he would be prepared to go across the north of Scotland, look at it and, if it was worth having, buy it and bring it back to Mallaig. He set off as the last snows of the winter were falling and made a deal. He loaded the mighty engine and generator onto the trailer and headed back west along Loch Ness towards Fort William.

Two days later we received a message via Mallaig that the expedition had broken down near Loch Ness, the big car overheating with the load. I sent Mitch off with my Mini and trailer to find the army party. I 'ordered' Mitch not to come back to Mallaig without the generator. I told him not to call me, just get out there and fetch the electricity! Two days later, towing the massive piece of machinery behind my little Mini, Mitch reappeared at Mallaig. He had had burst tyres and other problems, but the generator was almost home. We took it to Macintyres, the diesel engineers in the town, who looked at it in amazement.

'Well, Tom,' said the chief engineer, 'it's already done forty years' work so is there any point in taking it up the loch?'

But when they checked it over, they found nothing wrong. We now had to get it to Ardintigh by boat, our little 18-footer powered by the 5-horsepower Seagull outboard. We took the centre seat out of the boat and laid two railway sleepers along the floor from bow to stern. Then we lowered the generator into the boat. *Moby Dick* sank almost to the gunwales, but she floated, just. She looked a little like one of the famous Scottish puffer boats, a small structure with a massive engine in the middle.

We were lucky. It was a flat calm day but the trip took me more than three hours and we still had the problem of unloading the generator at Ardintigh. We had no crane or sheerlegs, just manpower. The machinery weighed about 1¼ tons. It was high tide, so I took the boat as close inshore as I could, having laid timbers on the stone foreshore to support her as the tide dropped. So far, so good.

There only seemed to be one answer to the problem of getting the engine ashore. Take it to pieces. I was surprised, on reflection, that we had not thought of that before leaving Mallaig; it would have made the little boat safer if the wind had risen during the trip round the headland and up the loch. We set to, taking off the two big flywheels, the cylinder head, removing the cylinder casing and the generator from the base mounting. While we were doing this two people appeared walking along the shore. Normally, in a whole year, we never see more than half a dozen people at Ardintigh who are not something to do with the camp, so it was quite a surprise, especially so early in the year. They came over towards the boat.

'Excuse me,' one of them asked, 'is this the Tarbert ferry to Mallaig?'

'No,' I replied, 'Tarbert's round the corner, a mile and a half or so that way and the ferry, the mail boat, doesn't come until tomorrow, Friday.'

They looked very crestfallen. The mail boat only came to Donald's lonely post office to deliver and collect mail, usually mine, on Mondays and Fridays, bringing the occasional passengers or holidaymakers using the trip as a cruise round the loch in summer.

'I'll tell you what I'll do,' I said, having one of my rare brainwaves. 'You help us unload this wee engine onto the beach and I'll feed you and then take you in the boat to Mallaig.'

They cheered up until they saw the engine.

Five hours later we were still carrying bits up the beach; seven hours later, in the evening, all was safely ashore. Our exhausted visitors had a clean-up and I gave them a McClean special, a slap-up curry, one of my staple meals in those early days in Scotland. Later that evening, as darkness fell, I took two replete, exhausted and very surprised walkers to Mallaig. We never saw them again at Ardintigh.

When Mitch and I were on our own we lived in a rough, simple way. We worked on the camp, caught lobsters, cooked an evening meal of beans or stew, and listened to the portable radio. There was no proper water supply, no washing facilities except the stream running down from the hills, or the sea. We had no electricity until I had sorted out and reassembled the generator, and then not until I wired up the huts. While the septic tank was being built, we had no modern lavatory, just an army-style pit. I couldn't afford proper oilskin clothing until later, every penny going on the huts, the boat, the lobster pots and the other essentials for the camp. Our comforts came second, although we had moved from the tent to one of the huts, basic though it was. We lined the huts with insulation and I used an old ammunition box dug into the burn to feed a header tank with fresh water which then was piped to the hut designated to be the cook house. The overflow from this became our shower, providing freezing cold water for an all-over wash. They were good days and we were never without something to do, be it clearing bracken, moving boulders from the approach to the beach, building a stone base for the generator or maintaining the boat.

8 The Army Arrive

On one of my infrequent trips south to the Venns I had met General Sir Cecil Blacker, known to his friends as Monkey. He had heard I was at the farm, which was near his home, and came round to ask if I would like a game of squash. He was a great person, enthusiastic and very keen to hear about the adventure centre. He suggested that as it was already popular with those soldiers who had 'discovered' it, I should write to the various district officers responsible for physical training. Help and suggestions like this, given in an informal but semi-professional way, was very encouraging, so I settled down and prepared the letters, describing the facilities at the centre and explaining that, with the huts and tents which they would bring themselves, I could take thirty-four men for a week at a time on a self-catering basis. I did not hide the fact that conditions were still very spartan, but we had already started to build the stone house that is today known as the Cave.

We began the construction of the Cave by making a base of local stone and concrete. Then we built dry-stone walls, forming a large rectangle, with a doorway facing the loch and gaps for windows. On top of this we put a flat sloping roof. It was to be an accommodation house to provide a sleeping place for eighteen men. I bought government-surplus two-tiered bunks and mattresses and waited for the army to arrive. I was looking forward to the reaction of the soldiers to the

Cave, the Ardintigh Hilton. In winter, with gale-force winds and high tides, the sea sweeps right into the door of the Cave. There was also one small wooden hut for the officers and another for the sergeants and NCOs who came as instructors with each group. We were open for business and business was on the way.

During the first summer, 1971, we had fifteen weeks booked by various army parties. They would either arrive at Mallaig in their own transport or travel by train to the ferry terminal which serves the Hebridean islands. They were totally independent, organizing their own activities and recreation. I would introduce them to the centre, show them the ropes, point out the local landmarks and then leave them to it. This meant that I was able to make one or two visits south to see the Venns and meet the general, who was delighted to hear that his idea had helped me and, at the same time, received the approval of the physical training officers. Mitch was my second in command, if you like. One of us was always there when the army was staying. We had an advisory role, only joining in climbs and walks either when we wanted to or when the soldiers suggested it.

One of the first units to use the centre came from the Royal Irish Rangers. They brought 290 men, including cooks in smart white hats and officers' stewards. Not only that, they also brought the officers' mess silver. They camped in two-man tents. All their kit had to be brought round from Mallaig by boat. The soldiers walked from the town, three miles along the road to Morar village and then up the track that runs north of Loch Morar, before cutting over the hills behind Ardintigh for the last few miles on a rough hill path which drops down into the camp from the south, twelve miles in all.

With groups such as these it became apparent that I needed a bigger boat for stores and for bringing the men from Mallaig. *Sea Otter*, the boat which we had used to shift the huts, was just what I needed. She was wooden, clinker-built, 26 feet long, with an inboard engine. She was for sale, at £1600, a high price for a boat like that. However, in the Highlands one cannot be as selective as one can be farther south where the market for secondhand boats is much larger. I reckoned the boat was worth about £1200, but it would have cost me the £400 difference to go south, find another boat, and bring it back to Ardintigh, so I really had little choice.

I bought her. She had a two-cylinder Lister diesel engine and was in good shape. I do not think I did too badly; she served me well for the next eight years while *Moby Dick* became the safety boat for the canoeing expeditions. I had bought some canoes in England, but they were not strong enough for the tasks carried out by the army so I went to Clive Freshwater, at Aviemore, who specialized in boats for shooting the rapids in the Scottish and Welsh rivers. I called them the battleships, they were so strong, but they could survive anything that the soldiers threw at them and wintered out in the Cave.

When buying *Sea Otter* I had asked several local friends what they thought of the boat and had chewed over their advice. By now I had made some good friends locally, but this was mostly thanks to advice given to me by David Stirling. He told me to go cannily, not to push my southern accent and to pay my bills on time! The Highlanders take a year or two, maybe longer, to accept a newcomer, but once they have accepted you as one of their own, they are the kindest, warmest friends you could ever hope to meet. If they don't accept you, then you might as well pack up and go back to the south or wherever you come from. Having said that, the Highlanders and Islanders are forgiving people, always prepared to accept someone as a friend rather than reject him, but even so it takes a long time before all the doors are opened. They had every reason to think I was just another madman on the run from the real world, but as the centre grew I began to notice passing boats slow a little as they looked at the huts, the Cave, the clearing on the beach and bracken.

Several things may have helped break the ice. First, my name, McClean. Secondly, my transatlantic rowing trip, though they thought I was crazy to have done it. Everyone on the west coast, bar a few, is connected with the sea, be they fishermen, ferry crews or in the fish marketing or marine engineering business. I said little or nothing about the rowing trip and was quite embarrassed when the word spread round the local villages about my voyage.

9 Further Adventures?

Itchy feet were becoming a problem again. The centre was chugging along at full steam with army teams taking up between twenty and twenty-five weeks of the year; a few smaller groups of civilians were coming for stays of three or four weeks, dotted through the season. I was running out of things to do.

Several ideas were going through my mind. One, the strongest, was to climb Mount Everest on my own. I had already started designing the Moby house box. This was a box 6 feet long, 3 feet wide and 3 feet high. Such boxes could be dropped on the mountain at various heights, ten of them, one at every 1000 feet from a base camp at 12,000 feet. In them would be stores, oxygen, spare climbing gear and clothing, and a relay radio. I could live in one of the boxes until the weather allowed me to move on to the next one. I bought plans and maps of the mountain, read books about it and did other research. I was really keen to give it a try and began training in the winter on the mountains around Ardintigh, at the same time writing to one or two people for advice. It was then the bombshell landed on my plan. There was a waiting list of people wanting to climb Everest. You have to register your climb with the Nepalese government and then, if the authorities approve your plans, wait for a slot. I was not keen to join a queue to climb a mountain, so while continuing to wire the camp for electricity, and put in the plumbing for the lavatories and hot showers, linking them to the septic tank, I thought out other ideas.

What about the South Pole? I had first read about Captain Scott's famous journey while I was at the training depot at Aldershot. Now I read again the descriptions of his various expeditions, especially the last one in which he and his companions died in their attempt to beat the Norwegian explorer Roald Amundsen to the Pole. They had camped for a winter on the edge of the Antarctic before establishing camps along their route. I made notes to assess where they had gone wrong. Many people will already know the answers. They took ponies, not dogs. Their sledges were too heavy to be towed by men once the ponies had reached the end of their endurance. Their food and stores, tents and sleeping equipment were heavy and cumbersome. The sleeping bags probably weighed as much as 30 lb each, their sledges alone about 80 lb, and their food was tinned, heated by heavy paraffin stoves.

I began to make lists of equipment for my solo journey. I would take a modern 10-lb sleeping bag, dehydrated food, gas to cook with, specially chosen so that it would not freeze in the Antarctic, and lightweight thermal clothing. Maybe I would take two dogs; they are almost self-sufficient, can pull for long distances, and can be eaten in a real emergency. I also began to design the Moby house sledge.

This was a lightweight sledge made of alloy and on it a cabin in which I could sleep. It seemed crazy to tow a sledge and then unload a tent, which would have to be erected, when I could live aboard the sledge and save the weight of the tent. The sledge itself would be 9 feet long, perhaps longer. The longer the sledge the easier it is for one man to pull. At the front would be an extension pole so that if I fell into a crevasse, I would be saved. The total length of the sledge and the pole would straddle the crevasse like a bridge, and I would be suspended below in the parachute-type harness with which I towed the sledge. Then, with lines, crampons and one-way sliding clips, I could haul myself back to the top.

One idea that I began to put to the test was to build part of the sledge out of concentrated dehydrated meat or even soya extract. Modern composite foods can be made harder than wood, so why should they not replace wood and be available if needed? Some people may raise an eyebrow at the idea of me trekking across the frozen wastes munching away at my transport, but the more I thought about it the more sense the idea seemed to make. Why spend energy pulling a sledge weighing, say, 50 lb just to carry food weighing 20 lb when the weight of food could be an integral part of the sledge? The sledge would weigh 500 lb loaded, hard to pull in heavy going, but it should glide along in reasonable conditions. Powdered snow would present a problem when it crystallized, but four wheels attached to the bottom of the runners would overcome this. I tried it on soggy sand and it worked.

I studied maps and charts of the Antarctic, read any books that I could find about modern Arctic expeditions and dreamed of frozen wastes. I knew that with the right planning I could do it. I wanted a success, not a heroic failure. I planned to start from McMurdo Sound, where Scott had set out on his journey to the Pole.

I studied the problems of navigation on the southern icecap which covers the Antarctic land mass. The compass is difficult to use down there because the variations caused by the earth's magnetic field are enormous, almost 180° in some places. To go south, one has to follow the compass bearing pointing almost north. I could obtain aerial and satellite pictures of the route and compare these with the maps, so much of my navigation, given reasonable visibility, would be by sight and dead reckoning.

I wrote to the British Antarctic Survey headquarters at Cambridge, explaining my plan and asking for advice. They were not at all pleased, giving me the firm impression that not only did they operate in the Antarctic, but they had invented it and owned it. They did not welcome solitary explorers roving around their patch, pointing out that if I became stuck in the middle of nowhere they would be the ones who would have to come and get me out. I accepted their point, but I regarded the trip to the Antarctic in the same way as the transatlantic row. If I got myself into trouble, I would have to get myself out. If I disappeared, I wouldn't expect anyone to go out of his way to spend time and money looking for me.

After my rebuff by the British Antarctic Survey, I spoke to David Stirling, who contacted the Americans. They had a base at McMurdo Sound but could not help. All routes to the subcontinent seemed to be failing. No one wanted to accept a lone explorer. Prince Harald of Norway, who had heard of my plan, offered training facilities in the Norwegian Arctic, but there was little point in accepting his offer if the final target was being blocked from view.

All in all, as the centre grew from strength to strength in popularity with the army, I spent almost two years trying to mount my two proposed expeditions, Everest first and the South Pole second. It cost me time and money. I wrote hundreds of letters but they came to nothing. I think there was, and still is, too much red tape around designed to stop people doing something adventurous. I often wonder what would have happened if I had decided to build my adventure centre in the south or southwest of England. Planning permission and other restrictions would have probably killed it dead before I had even found the land. However, in Scotland, although it was a struggle at first to obtain planning permission, it eventually came through. Life seems to become more and more complicated all the time. It's sad.

I am very patriotic, probably because of my time in the army, so I was furious when I heard that a Japanese bloke had reached the North Pole alone, using American satellite navigation systems to find his way there. I admired him, but it made me seethe that my effort had, in the main, been baulked by British officialdom. I would love to see a Briton reach the South Pole alone, and would love it even more if it was me.

To me adventure is part of life and comes in a wide variety of ways: climbing Everest, walking to the South Pole, or crossing the ocean alone. Risk has no real part in adventure. Planning has. Racing drivers may be regarded by some as adventurers, and perhaps they are, but they face risk, unavoidable risk sometimes, and that, to me, is not acceptable.

However, there are other sorts of adventure. Painting a

picture for the first time counts as an adventure for me. I started painting at Ardintigh. It was General Sir Cecil Blacker who put me on the right track during our games of squash and long talks when I was down at the Venns'. I was not sure whether I had the skill, but there was no better way to find out than to try. When in Inverness for a shopping visit, I went to an art shop and asked for the basic essentials. The people at the shop were very helpful and I was soon on my way home, raring to begin my first masterpiece. Nothing less would do.

I used to get very cross with myself if the picture did not turn out right. I would try again and again until it was. When I had mastered the basics, I moved on to something else. I am no great artist, but I taught myself to paint what I saw and was delighted when a friend asked if he could have one of my paintings as a souvenir of his stay at Ardintigh. At the time this was almost as great a success as crossing the ocean or starting the old generator after all the battles to get it installed. When the first glimmer of light appeared in the bulbs in the huts, that was another achievement which I rated as an adventure in its own way.

Ardintigh was a grand place to start a hobby like painting. When alone there, I became very inward looking, introspective; painting was a way of getting out of myself. It was also a fine excuse to stop the heavy work of shifting stones and gathering sand from across the loch which I was going to use for rebuilding the croft. Most of my works were wild seascapes taken from around Mallaig, or scenes from my imagination – the Antarctic, the oceans. I painted one picture of Sir Ernest Shackleton's boat, the *James Caird*, in which he and a small party sailed from Elephant Island in the South Shetlands to South Georgia, 300 miles away, to find help for the crew of the *Endurance* which had been stranded in ice and abandoned in the Weddell Sea.

Along with Scott, Shackleton was another of my heroes. Personally, having read everything I could find on both men, I feel that Shackleton was probably the greater of the two. I had his picture in the shelter of *Super Silver* during the transatlantic trip inscribed simply with the words 'The Boss'. I would see this picture last thing before going to sleep and first thing on waking. The story of his 1914–16 Antarctic expedition, when *Endurance* was trapped in ice floes for nine months, has never ceased to amaze and inspire me. Shackleton and his crew abandoned the crushed ship and towed two ship's boats, one the *James Caird*, across the Antarctic wastes, living on the ice in the upturned boats. Ernest Shackleton not only reached South Georgia to find help, but lost not one man from his entire crew in spite of failing three times to reach help. He and his boat's crew were eventually rescued by the Chilean tug *Yelcho*. I later presented my painting of his epic voyage in the small boat to the estate club at Inverie where it hangs to this day.

Painting was a therapy when alone at Ardintigh, but it also provided some income. Some of my work sold for as much as £50, which helped with the budget in those hard days.

10 Jill

Steve Mitchell was with me throughout those early days at Ardintigh. Although he had originally come for only a few months he stayed for almost five years. He had been a loyal, hard-working friend, sharing the discomforts and achievements. During those first winters we had lived like hermits, struggling to keep warm at night by resorting to lemonade bottles filled with hot water stuffed into our sleeping bags. But now, Mitch felt that he had done all he could at the camp; we had electricity, calor-gas cooking, and regular visits by teams of soldiers. I understood his attitude. After all, the place was mine and the fruits of all our efforts were mine in the long term. He had seen the growth of the clam-diving game in Loch Nevis and around Mallaig. Clams in Scotland are called scallops in the south, and the demand for them in the fish markets was intense. Mitch realized that he needed to earn some real money.

By this time another event had occurred that was a major turning point in my life. I had been over in Arisaig seeing friends. It was spring, 1974. The camp was humming with activity and my mind was on rebuilding the derelict croft into a proper house. As I drove towards the village I saw a girl walking along the road in the direction that I was driving. I stopped, offered her a lift and began talking to her. After dropping her off at the village store, Cnoc-na-Faire, which I nicknamed Nic-Knockies, I went back to my friends' house to find out more about her. Since moving to Scotland I had taken some notice of one or two girls, but never become very involved. It was that business of keeping at arm's length from the local people until they accepted me, and taking their daughters out was part of that. Out where? I could hardly take them back to Ardintigh; that would have caused a real scandal and probably led to a posse coming to get me and drive me out of Scotland.

News travels fast in the small Scottish communities. I was told that the girl who had caught my eye was called Jill Stacey, that she was on holiday from Yorkshire and was staying in the village at Arisaig. I called at the place where she was staying and asked her out for a drink that evening. She did not know it at the time, but I had my sights on her. She was a great girl, that was my first impression of her, and while we were not exactly all over each other, we talked for hours. She had a level head on her shoulders, talked a great deal of sense and had a wonderful sense of humour. I asked her for her home address, told her that I would call and see her when next in England, and went home feeling about six feet tall. She did not believe she would ever see me again.

I had to wait for almost the whole summer before I could go south on one of my visits to the Venns. On the way down I stopped at Wath-upon-Dearne, near Rotherham, found Jill's home and knocked on the door. She was amazed to see me, happy too, I think. We went out for the evening. The idea of marriage was already bubbling up in my mind, certainly as I continued my journey south.

We did not see much of each other during that first year, but kept in touch. I went down to Yorkshire for short holidays and Jill visited Ardintigh, hardly able to believe that someone could build a place like that miles from anywhere. It was a far cry from the life she was used to in the streets and homes of comfortable Yorkshire. Most people, before deciding to marry, spend time getting to know each other. Often they come from similar backgrounds. We had a problem there. It was vital for Jill to be sure that she would be happy at Ardintigh, not just on the fine summer days but in winter when a northerly gale was sweeping down the loch, driving snow before it. The nearest shop was one hour away by boat or at the end of a three-hour walk over steep hills and peat bogs.

Apart from the urge to break free, I think that Mitch felt left out of Ardintigh life now that I was spending more and more time with Jill, either there or, when possible, in the south. He found a job diving for clams with Rob Foster who had come up from England, bought a small fishing boat, *The Twig*, and started diving successfully.

In 1975, about a year after we first met, I asked Jill to marry me and she agreed. Ardintigh had passed the test, and so, apparently, had I. I was very happy, but we decided to wait before getting married. The croft had to be rebuilt, but working alone it would take time. From when we became engaged in 1975 until we married in 1976 I battled on. Even so it was clear that we were likely to start married life in winter in one of the huts with just a paraffin stove for heat and the ammunition box up in the burn for a shower.

After Mitch left I had some long periods on my own. Between visits from Jill and the army units, my days were spent lobster fishing, constructing a pier in the centre of the beach, and, of course, rebuilding the croft. It had been abandoned for years, the last people to use it being fishermen who, back in the 1930s, would come ashore to camp there and cook meals. The place had caught fire and been almost destroyed. Once fire has damaged a stone building, the stones and mortar between them are weakened, so I had to start from scratch, putting in hogging, loose stones, as a foundation with a concrete floor on top. It was hard work. The sand for the concrete had to be loaded in plastic fertilizer sacks on the other side of the loch where there was a good sandy beach and humped across to my side, twenty at a time. Each weighed about half a hundredweight. Apart from that, there was the tree which had grown up inside the walls to a height of 40 feet. It had to be cut down and the roots completely dug out. My early experience on the building sites had given me a basic knowledge of house construction, but I had no training in plumbing or electricity. Those skills I learned as I went along.

It was during one of these solitary times that I almost lost

Sea Otter. I had returned alone to Ardintigh after a trip south, arriving at the mooring off the beach as it was getting dark. Because of this I decided to leave the suitcase on board which, among other things, contained my best suit. I made sure that the boat was properly secured, climbed into the dinghy and rowed ashore. There was a bit of a breeze blowing, but nothing to worry about as I made a meal and went to bed for a good night's sleep. Next morning I woke early and looked out across the loch. No boat. I pulled on my clothes and boots and set off, first along the shoreline to the west and then to the east, round the point towards Tarbert. Still no boat. I sat on the foreshore looking across the loch, although I could think of no way that *Sea Otter* could have set out northwards against the breeze and tide.

As I sat staring at the place the mooring was meant to be, I realized that it, too, had disappeared. The mooring buoy had gone. I leaped into the dinghy, grabbing a grappling line and hook as I went, and rowed out to where the boat should have been. I trailed the hook in the water and hit something first time. Almost falling out of the dinghy, I heaved on the line. Something beneath the surface moved upwards, inch by inch. Little by little I took in more line, not believing my luck. I looked over the side of the dinghy and saw the pulpit, on the bow of the boat, below the surface. The bow was pointing straight upwards. I slashed the line between the boat and the mooring.

There I was, a hundred yards off the beach in a small dinghy anchored to the seabed by a two-ton launch. It seemed that the mooring buoy, the air trapped in the forrard cabin and other buoyancy in the hull was just about counter-balancing the weight of the non-floating parts of the boat.

I began to row towards the beach, inching my way in. Then the stern of the sunken boat, 26 feet down, hit the bottom and became stuck. I took the bow rope of the dinghy, tied it to my waist and jumped into the sea, swimming for all I was worth. The line from the dinghy to the bow of the sunken boat would not allow me to reach the beach so I went ashore for a longer line and an anchor.

Frantically I worked to connect the bow of the boat to the longer line and then, once the anchor was buried on the beach, I began working the boat towards the shore as the tide rose, lifting it off the bottom. It took a long hard time to pull the boat as close as possible to the land at high water. All I could do then was wait for the tide to drop, leaving the boat stranded.

As the tide began to fall again, I went aboard and dived into the little forrard cabin to remove any heavy objects and my kit. To my horror I realized that not only was my one and only suit among the sodden mass, but also my photo albums. I carried them up the beach and unpacked the case. The sun was out and a good breeze was blowing, so I spread the photos out on the grass. Then I stuffed the arms and legs of the suit with dead bracken and hung it up in a tree, like a scarecrow, to dry. All was not lost but it was a mess.

I returned to the boat and dived once more, looking for the bung in the bottom of the hull. It took several dives to find it and several more to release it, but at last the water started running out. I waited for it to drain away and then found the reason for the sinking. There was a pump toilet in the bow. Someone had forgotten to close the inlet valve after using the toilet. As the boat lay to the mooring, rising and falling head to wind, water had gradually slopped into the toilet basin and overflowed inside the boat until it was level with the top of the pan which was set quite low in the bow cabin. Once that happened the sea simply flooded slowly in, filling the boat. I had learned a lesson, but wondered how many other boats had been sunk that way.

Once the boat was drained I set about drying the engine. All the engine oil had floated out so I filled the entire engine with paraffin to prevent damage from rusting and to wash out the sea water. It took a long time to be sure that the engine was quite free from water before I could refill it with engine oil. Next I had to drain the fuel system and the injectors that supply the fuel to the cylinders. That done, I swung the engine over for several minutes. First one cylinder fired and then the other. The engine was working and the tide was coming in again at the end of what had been a long wasted day.

Next I had to recover the mooring line out in the bay and reattach the line that I had cut. When the boat was afloat I took her out into the loch to check that all was working and secured her to the mooring, making doubly sure that the seacocks were all shut. Damage to the boat was minimal, but it took several days before the cabin dried out.

When Mitch decided to go off on his own, I had to find an assistant to replace him. I needed someone to work as a boatman and help run the camp, particularly on the occasions when I was away. I placed advertisements in several newspapers and applications flooded in. We sifted through the replies and asked a few people to come for an interview. This did not always turn out to be a matter of a simple chat. Some of them took one look at the remoteness of the place and made up their own minds. They left. We finally chose Ron Fayers. He was a great character, nicknamed Mad Ron by those who came to know him. This was not an insult, but a reflection of the eccentric things he would do just for the sheer hell of it.

Ron joined Ardintigh in the early part of 1976 and soon showed us the character that he was. I sent him off to Mallaig in the big boat to collect a load of stores brought up by one of the army units. He came back with about half, so I gave him a good talking to, told him to get a grip on himself. It was a wet day, rain sheeting along the loch, but he went back. Most of the remaining stores consisted of cartons of beer cans. The rain had soaked the cardboard containers and as the soldiers threw the boxes into the boat, about 10,000 cans in all, the cartons split. Ron came back to Ardintigh with the boat almost sinking, beer cans heaped right above the gunwales. He seemed quite pleased with himself so I told him that he had done well, not adding that he had, in fact, done very well not to have lost the boat.

On another occasion, when I was away, he went across to Inverie in a full southwesterly gale with young Neil Trotter, who, during school holidays, used to come to Ardintigh to help us. Neil's father was the engineer on the Knoydart estate and the family were great friends of mine. The wind was screaming up the loch straight towards the shore on the north side of the loch. The villagers saw Ron coming and almost the entire population went to the small pier to wave him off as it was far too dangerous to attempt a landing. He got the message and with Neil at the helm headed back for Ardintigh.

Now, one of my fetishes is keeping the boats clean and shipshape, ropes coiled, everything properly stowed and no loose gear lying about. Ron knew this and would straighten the boats out from time to time. He chose this moment, in a full gale, to tidy the boat, throwing odd plastic bags over the side and generally having a good sort-out. Unfortunately, two of the bags contained Neil's kit, spare jerseys, jeans and dry clothing. It was all lost in the storm.

Another time, again when I was away, he went to Mallaig to fetch army kit and a loading party of men, about eight in all. It was a warm sunny day and as the boat rounded the point at the top of the Mallaig peninsula Ron suddenly left the helm, took all his clothes off and jumped into the sea, leaving the boat heading up the loch. The amazed soldiers did not, at that stage, know who Ron was. He could have been me so far as they were concerned. Eventually one of them, who knew a little about boats, stepped forward and took the wheel, turning the boat back to where Ron, now several hundred yards away, was splashing about naked in the sea. They picked him up and, announcing that it was a good day for a swim, he clambered aboard, dressed and took them on to the camp, still bemused by this strange wild man.

At about the time when Ron joined Ardintigh, new friends whom I call the Fun People, began coming to Loch Nevis. The uncle of theatrical producer Cameron Mackintosh had come to Mallaig after he retired as a tea planter in the Far East. He had set up Greaves's carpentry shop in Mallaig and then retired for a second time to a log cabin up on the loch side at Tarbert, across the small bay from Donald and Jessie's post office. Cameron would go there for his holidays as a boy and when his uncle died he became the trustee of the log cabin and the land on which it stood. He brought a really mixed collection of friends up to the cabin during the summer months, the first group arriving during the scorching summer of 1976.

They were a complete contrast to those we normally saw at Ardintigh and Tarbert, where the emphasis was on outdoor activities and fitness, but we soon made friends with them, one group contrasting with the other. It was not that they did not enjoy or appreciate the surroundings, but their approach was different. For them Tarbert was an escape, a relaxation, from town life and the business world of the south, where most of them lived. Certainly they would climb the hills, come out on the boats and enjoy the Highlands, but they were not looking for a challenge, rather finding peace and quiet, making their own entertainment and generally not being tied to routines. The Fun People, it was a good name that I found for them, because that is exactly what they were.

Cameron has recently earned fame as the producer of the musical *Cats*. Phil Rhodes became a particular friend. He was an adventurer, having sailed the Atlantic and run yachts in the West Indies. Perhaps it would be fair to say that he was something of an adventurer in business as well, always prepared to take a gamble or risk where others would have had second thoughts. There was also Trevor Moore, in the printing business, another person who still remains a good friend, Dave Witney, who was in property, and Robert Dewynter, a London businessman, known to us as the Mad Major. Most of them came from London or the Haslemere area in Surrey.

They would live off the land, bringing quantities of good wine and other drinks to enjoy with the scallops or lobsters that would appear as if by magic in the evenings. One delicacy, a new experience for me, was coquilles St Jacques, scallops cooked in cream and cheese sauce. Every meal at Tor-an-albanaich, as the house was called, was a new adventure to me after my simple way of life in which a steak cooked on an open fire was a treat.

I remember one evening when we had been over to the club at Inverie for a few drinks before heading back to Cameron's croft for dinner. The wind was piping up as we headed back from the club, but it was nothing to worry about. We reached Tarbert, helping Donald and Jessie, who had come with us, ashore before putting the boat on the mooring. Then we went in to eat dinner. Robert's wife Helen had cooked a dish which involved boning several different birds and then cooking them one stuffed inside the other. It was a superb meal, but all the while the wind was rising. By one o'clock in the morning, when it was time to be going back to Ardintigh, I thought of staying at the log cabin for the night. I had not seen such seas in the loch in summer and Ron, who had obviously enjoyed the evening as much as I had, was quite pleased at the idea of staying there for the night. However, I decided that we should go back to Ardintigh, just a short hop down the loch. Ron's face fell. My reason for this decision was that the mooring in the creek at Tarbert was not as strong and heavy as that at Ardintigh.

It really was blowing a hummer as we put out in the dinghy for the mooring and clambered aboard *Sea Otter*. It was as black as pitch, scarcely a glimmer of light, as we dropped the Tarbert mooring and headed out into the loch and then towards Ardintigh bay. My big flashlight had been lost in the earlier sinking but we had a torch. We kept going, taking half an hour for a trip that normally takes ten minutes. At last we found the mooring. I told Ron to get on the bow and grab the buoy as I took the boat past it; if he felt he was going over the side he was to let the mooring go and we would have another try. I also advised him that if he did fall over the side he should stay calm and let the wind carry him towards the shore, for it was blowing at about 50 knots straight from the northwest.

We made one try, missed and went round again. This time Ron picked up the buoy and hauled in. I ran from the wheel and grabbed him round the waist while he pulled, finally pulling with him. We threw the line round the samson post on the bow and collapsed in a heap for a few seconds. Perhaps I would have been wiser to have gone back to the shelter of Tarbert Bay. It was too late now, we were home, almost. We secured the boat and made our way to the stern to climb into the small dinghy.

We paddled ashore in what I call Hawaiian Five O style, side by side, one paddle each. Rowing was impossible because in the small boat one rower would impede the other. We had not managed more than a few strokes when a monster wave, far bigger than the others, swept in from the loch and picked up the dinghy like so much driftwood. We were thrown forward like a pair of dolls, landing in the sea with the dinghy on top of us. We clung on to the small boat and drifted towards the shore, probably as fast as we had been rowing. We arrived on the beach in the surf, sopping wet but glad to be alive and on the stone beach. We dragged the dinghy to the grass and helped each other up the field towards the beginnings of the house.

Ron was already living in the house, such as it was, sleeping on planks under the rafters. By now, with marriage pressing, I had managed to put a roof on the place and had fitted dormer windows, but it was still uninhabitable unless one was like Ron. He could live anywhere and enjoy it.

I said goodnight to him as he headed into the house and made my way to the hut that I was using as my home, collapsing into bed in a sodden heap, having stripped off my soaking clothes. It was almost two hours since we had left the cheerful party at Tor-an-albanaich. The storm continued to rage outside, but I slept the sleep of an exhausted man, waking, as usual, with the first beams of the early sun as they made their way over the high hills to the east of Ardintigh. I found some dry clothes and opened the door of the hut. God! There was the launch lying on her side high and dry on the edge of the beach. She was obviously damaged.

'Ron! Ron!' I screamed. 'Get up, quick!' I ran down the beach towards the boat, fearing the worst. She was surely a wreck. Ron emerged from his eyrie in the rafters of the incomplete croft. I was rushing round in a state of desperation and Ron in a state of sympathy.

'Get the Fun People,' I said. 'Get over to the log cabin and ask them to come and help, quick, before the tide comes in again!'

He ambled off along the seashore towards Tarbert while I rushed around looking for boat-mending tools and materials. The party from the log cabin did not hurry themselves. They had their breakfast and then came round, four or five of them, ready to help with emergency repairs so that I could take the boat back down the loch to Mallaig for proper repairs at a boatbuilder's yard.

The boat was smashed in along one side so I dug out the rocks from under the damaged planks and we nailed new timber over the broken wood. Then we tacked canvas over the new wood and painted it with pitch. Inside we built struts right across the boat to support the broken frames. We drained the engine, flushed it through with cleansing oil and, once it started, sailed round to the shelter of the beach at Tarbert to beef up the repairs.

Phil Rhodes took care of the insurance for me, but by the time that word came through that the insurance company would pay for professional repairs, the Fun People had all gone back south. I managed to persuade a reluctant Donald to help me take the boat to Mallaig to the boatbuilders. He was right to be apprehensive. Once we left the shelter of Tarbert the leaks started; we were bailing with a bucket the whole way to Mallaig, a long hour and a half which left us exhausted, but we made it.

It was after that sensational summer of 1976, in October, that I went to Yorkshire for my wedding. Jill and I were married in the church at Wath-upon-Dearne, Jill's side of the church packed with her many relatives while the general deputized as my father. The Venns came up from the south to add their support and blessings, and Auntie Kay came over from Ireland with her son, 'cousin' Adrian, and his wife Audrey. We had a good wedding reception in Doncaster and then set off to Benidorm, in Spain, for the honeymoon.

Benidorm! What a place after Ardintigh! I was like a fish out of water among the sky-rise hotels, disco bars and instant entertainment. The weather was not what I had expected, either, but Jill seemed happy as we took several sightseeing tours. She had, for once, got me on her terms; I would rather have spent our honeymoon in a less overcivilized place, perhaps on safari in Africa. We came home and made our way back to Ardintigh to face our first winter there. Ron left in September, so we were on our own.

Through the depths of winter we lived together in my hut, 20 feet long by 10 feet wide, with only a double bed, a television that worked off the generator, a desk with my paints on it and some carpet. The cookhouse was across the field as was the toilet block. It was a very cold winter. Washing in the burn in the snow was the exact opposite of a baptism of fire for Jill – a baptism of ice and snow!

I was busy trying to make the house fit to live in. There was flooring to be put in and I can remember Jill helping line the chimney with cement. I stood on the top of the chimney while she filled the buckets below ready for me to hoist. It was backbreaking work, but it kept us warm and Jill seemed to become happier and happier with Ardintigh and our way of life as time went by.

We continued to carry sand from across the loch in order to make what to me seemed to be an endless supply of cement and concrete, loading the safety boat to the gunwales and making our way slowly and carefully home.

One of our worst moments was after *Sea Otter* had been repaired. We went in her to Mallaig to collect timber for the house. The weather was not too bad on the trip down the loch and nothing worse had been forecast, so we loaded the boat as full as we dared and set out for home. In spite of the shipping forecast, the wind increased as we headed into the loch, passing the headland that marks the halfway point of the journey. The boat was taking quite a quantity of water, more, I feared, than the hand-operated pump could cope with, but I pumped away, deciding to head for Inverie to try to escape the worst of the wind and therefore the waves.

We hit some bad seas, the whole boat leaping from the water and crashing back again. Jill screamed, the only time I have known her show any real fear of the sea. I was worried; the normal time for the journey – an hour and a half or so – had already stretched to almost three hours and darkness was falling fast as the storm increased. We inched across the loch again, finding it impossible to escape the wind whichever way we went. Three and a half hours after leaving Mallaig we reached Ardintigh. I did not bother with moorings and dinghies but simply drove the boat straight onto the beach. Jill leaped into the surf, scampered up the beach and collapsed in a heap on the grass. The boat was half waterlogged, we were soaked to the skin and freezing cold. It had been a nightmare for Jill and a big worry for me. I backed the boat out into the bay again and found the mooring; it was too risky to leave *Sea Otter* on the beach. Half an hour and another battle later, I came ashore in the dinghy feeling beaten; the timbers would have to take their chance out there that night.

We had our first married Christmas in Yorkshire with Jill's

family, a welcome break for her. In March 1977 a detachment of soldiers from the Brigade of Guards arrived, our first visitors of the year, and we moved into the house. It was not really ready for habitation, but the roof was on and slated, the windows in and the flooring down. We had the essentials of a kitchen, a bedroom and lights. The room that is now our comfortable little sitting room was the workshop, while the second bedroom sufficed as a sitting room. Our furniture was being stored by a friend, Mrs Cameron-Head, at Loch Ailort Castle. It was another full year before the ground floor was covered with more than just concrete and the plastering completed. Jill was in charge of decorating, choosing the colours and curtains. I needed a woman's touch in my so far male-oriented life. Up to now one of my favourite colours had been khaki.

The army groups were bringing in enough money for us to live on, but I wanted to make more. Diving seemed to be the answer. The clam diving along the coast was reported to be very successful and the lobster fishing was spasmodic, the effort sometimes hardly worth the eventual reward. Wishing that I had decided to start diving for clams several years earlier, I studied the various diving methods being used by the people working from Mallaig. Most used air bottles and wet suits, charging the bottles on an air compressor aboard the boat. Others used an airline, 400 feet long, running from a compressor with a regulator to ensure a constant supply of air. The diver would take the line down with him and draw air from it as needed. This was the method I opted for and I set off to buy the kit, which cost nearly £1000.

Jill was apprehensive about the idea and her mother almost forbade it completely when she heard about my plan. I had not had much experience of diving, having done only a little when in Malaya, from the causeway that links Singapore to the mainland. To keep Jill happy, before fitting the compressor and other kit into the boat, I set the rig up on the shore, laid out the airline, put on the wet suit and prepared for a dive from the beach. When I first tried out the wet suit I was very buoyant in spite of carrying a weight-belt round my waist, a canvas belt with pockets fitted with lumps of lead. I was a little nervous and this meant that I instinctively filled my lungs with too much air, puffing my chest up. That problem solved itself after a dive or two, but at first I could not stay below the surface. The answer was staring me in the face on the beach. I picked up a bloody great rock in my arms, about 20 lb in weight, and walked into the sea. It worked. At about 20 feet down I relaxed and began to enjoy the experience. The wet suit, made of neoprene, traps water in hundreds of tiny cells between the outer skin of the suit and one's body, the water being warmed by body heat. It works, even in winter, though there were times, I admit, when it was very cold out there in the loch.

I experimented from the beach, going farther out and exploring the bottom, gaining confidence all the time. Once the compressor was in the boat it was time to start working out in the loch. Jill, and one or two other people, asked me what would happen if the compressor engine failed. This was not really a problem because there would be enough air left in the airline to give me at least a minute of air, time enough to reach the surface. I always checked and double checked all my kit before diving, especially the fuel, one of the commonest causes of a compressor motor stopping.

We loaded all our bits and pieces onto *Sea Otter*, coiled the airline up on the stern and set out into the loch. The best clams were out on the reefs and shelves in the deeper water, but I decided to start by working right round the shore of the loch. Success came quickly, often in the least expected places. When diving past the narrows towards the head of the loch I managed to lift more than 1150 clams.

I averaged about two days' diving a week, interspersed with trips to the market and work around the camp on the buildings and general maintenance. Later, as the work ashore became less demanding, I dived as many as four days a week, but this was partly because the price of clams was dropping while they were becoming harder to find.

A typical diving day began with an early start and a good breakfast. Jill steered the boat out to a selected spot while I pulled on my suit. Ideally, I could manage three dives a day, allowing for decompression time between the dives. Once in the area where I wanted to dive I cruised around with the echo sounder running to find a reef on which the clams would be lying. Once over the reef I dropped anchor and stopped the main engine, started the compressor and checked the air supply. Jill had a watch to time the length of the dive. I could stay at 100 feet for about eighteen minutes and then needed about two hours to decompress before being able to go down again. At 60 feet I could stay under water a little longer and take less time between dives, so I tried to find reefs at that depth. Even then, I had to work fast once on the bottom.

I would start at the extremity of the airline from the boat and work to a spot under the boat. This saved Jill having to haul me back on the line when loaded with clams. The bags I took down with me carried as much as 150 lb once filled with the scallop shells, not a bad load under water as they had a certain amount of buoyancy, but they were a real load to heave into the boat. As I filled each bag with shells I fed air from the airline into a plastic container attached to the bag, keeping the air in the container just sufficient to support the bag but not enough to shoot it to the surface. Top up with twenty or so clams, add a little more air – it was a steady routine business. After twenty minutes, with luck, I would have a bag holding one and a half hundredweight of clams supported by a plastic container of air.

Once ready to go up I clipped a line from the airline to the bag and let it rise to the surface up the airline while I took my time coming up to avoid decompression problems, the bends. Once I was sure it was safe to surface, I came up near the boat, climbed aboard and we had a hot cup of tea, soup or coffee before I went down again.

In the early days of diving the boat was virtually open, with just a small cuddy, or cabin space, in the bow. There was no proper deck cabin. Once in the winter the boat was covered with about two inches of snow and a bitter east wind was sweeping down the loch. While I hopped over the side in my wet suit into the comparative warmth of the water Jill sat shivering on the open deck waiting and watching out for me, so we built a deck cabin and life improved at sea.

I enjoyed the diving, I still do, but it was important not to try to do too much. We were not allowed by law to take shells of less than 3½ inches across so there will always be clams there, but to make life easier I kept the shells that were too small for the market and dropped them overboard on the reef right in front of my own beach, ensuring a future supply on my own doorstep.

One day all my clam bags burst while lying on the bottom of Ardintigh bay. I had been fishing for them for two or three days, leaving each day's haul on the seabed near the camp so that they would stay fresh, ready to go to the market. We were going to leave the camp very early, sell the clams at the market and then go to Yorkshire for a week. But a storm had come up during the night and when I hauled up the bags, every single one had split.

There was only one thing to do. I pulled on my diving suit, started the compressor and began diving to recover the clams, about 500 of them, scattered over the seabed. No clams, no trip south, that was the rule that went through my mind as I worked. Three hours later they were all restowed in new bags. We set off for Mallaig, arranged for the clams to be sold and headed south.

One thing that had occurred to me was the need for some sort of base near Mallaig. I thought about it for some time and then heard that a showman's caravan was for sale in the area, a vast ornate affair with tinted glass, storage boxes under the floor sides and a flight of steps up to the door. It would mean that Jill and I would have somewhere to stay nearer shops and civilization, if one considers shops to be a contribution to the civilized world. As well as being a base near the village, it would serve as an office for the camp. I bought the van; it was already on a site at Angie MacLellan's house, Curtaig, at Morar just down the road from Mallaig. I also bought a speedboat, 17½ feet long, which I named *Colt 45* after the gun which had led to the near-fatal shooting accident in Greece all those years before. It was purely a 'fun boat', a bit of rare self-indulgence, for Jill and me to use for picnics on the loch and a quicker way to travel from Ardintigh to Mallaig and back.

Marriage had certainly cracked the ice with the locals. The solitary madman up the loch had now acquired a pretty girl whom they immediately took to. After our wedding the doors had really been thrown open in the most Highland of ways. The Knoydart estate gave a party for us at the estate club with a group from Fort William, Fergie Macdonald and his Highland Band. It was quite an occasion with everyone from the oldest inhabitant to the smallest children dancing the night away. People came from far and wide, some from far away across the loch by boat. The Highlands of Scotland must be one of the few places left in the world where people set out for an evening wearing their best suits or dresses – and wellington boots.

11 From Strength to Strength at Ardintigh

The summer of 1977 passed quickly, Jill managing to put a new meaning into my life and into Ardintigh as a place. It was no longer just a camp where I worked. It was a home of our own, the first time in my life that I really understood the meaning of the word. Certainly the Venns had shown me what home was all about, but that was still not quite the same. Almost every day Jill, by having a new view of Ardintigh, would open my eyes to a different aspect of the countryside and the people who lived there.

No one can consider himself an unofficial member of the Ardintigh club until he has climbed the mountain at the head of Loch Nevis, Sgùrr-na-Ciche, an impressive peak just 88 feet short of 3500 feet and steep. Normally those making the climb take an eight-mile walk along the south side of the loch before starting, but I wanted Jill to enjoy her first climb, not turn it into a commando training exercise so, as a concession, I told her that we would take *Sea Otter* to the loch head and climb from there. It was a warm summer's day, clear sky and fine for the expedition.

We set out in the morning, reached the beach at the top of the loch and started up the lower slopes, climbing boots, shorts and shirts being the kit, with me carrying a small backpack with light-weather protective clothing in case, though extremely unlikely that day, cloud or mist came in from the sea on the westerly wind. This is an essential rule in the Highlands, one which I never break. Too many people who do not understand the hills set off on a fine day in light summer clothes and, more often than not, useless light beach shoes. They end up suffering from exposure being brought down by mountain rescue teams or lifted off by helicopter.

Boots, with good ankle support, are essential in the Highlands or any hill country, worn with good clean dry wool socks. The soles of the boots should be well ribbed and not worn smooth. More accidents happen in the hills because of people wearing the wrong footwear – twisted and broken ankles, falls caused by slipping on wet grass or loose shale – than from any other cause.

We need not have worried that day, but we still took the right kit. By the time we were at the 1000-foot contour line I was carrying Jill's shirt and shorts in the pack and she was climbing in bikini and boots! Halfway up the mountain there is a small loch, a lochan, where we had a picnic and swam to cool off in the sweltering heat. Midges, always a problem in Scotland, are no bother when the sun is hot but clegs, big horse flies, are and we were bitten often, but this did not seem to deter Jill, doing her Highland streak.

We reached the top and sat for a long time looking at the view which I consider to be one of the finest in the Highlands. To the northwest the mountains of Skye, jagged, gnaw up to the sky while all around other peaks stretch away as far as the eye can see. After a rest and time for Jill to take in the beauty, we set off down again. I explained the map to her which, like the protective clothing, I always carry, and showed her how to follow a compass bearing. She grasped it all very quickly and was soon leading from landmark to landmark like a professional soldier.

Apart from learning the basic tricks of enjoying the hills and being able to survive in them, Jill began taking a firm hold on the secretarial work of the centre. She had worked as a secretary in Yorkshire, so knew how to take care of that side of business, where I was often almost out of my depth. She also decided that we should charge more per week to the units coming to the centre while keeping numbers down to a platoon, between twenty-four and thirty-six men including their officers and instructors. She also converted one hut which had been a store for the boat equipment and other essentials into a small camp shop, a mini-NAAFI. She stocked it with beer, cigarettes, chocolate, mint cake and basic needs like toothpaste, soap, cream for blisters, anti-midge cream and cans of soft drinks. Now, when the bell rings in the evening, it is to announce that the shop is open for business, a popular time with soldiers who have spent the day on the hills or out on the loch.

The secretarial effort paid off. Bookings by the army began to grow, mainly due to Jill's letters to an increasing number of training officers in the various regions. Usually each group intending to come to the centre first sends a reconnaissance party which arrives a month or so ahead of the course. This normally consists of the officer in charge and a senior sergeant who acts as instructor or second in command. They are shown the camp, the boats, the lie of the land and given a suggested routine for each day of the week that the group will be at Ardintigh. Almost without exception they accept these suggestions, which are based on my previous experience. One purpose of the recce, as I call it, is to show them just how remote the centre is. They are able to see the accommodation in the Cave and the huts; the cookhouse and other facilities, and decide what kit they will need.

Four or five weeks later the platoon of men arrives, usually by the overnight train from the south, at Mallaig. There is no doubt that eyebrows are raised as the soldiers look out of the train from Fort William while the big diesel engine roars away at the front of the small four-carriage train, hauling it up the single-track line cut out of mountain rock from Fort William, through places with magic names such as Glenfinnan, Arisaig and Morar.

Once at Mallaig they unload their kit and take it to the waiting boat at the quay in the fish harbour. Often they meet a departing group of soldiers who exaggerate the terrors of Ardintigh but certainly look as though they have been living rough in the hills. This, with a night of little sleep and a few beers or more on the long train ride via Glasgow, must surely cause a few qualms in young stomachs. It's a far cry from the Salisbury Plain and the tank ranges along England's south coast. The officer in charge selects a baggage party to travel up the loch with the kit and unload it at the other end. The rest, eyeing the steep hill behind Mallaig, prepare to walk in to Ardintigh. It is a hard walk, but a good introduction to the west coast of Scotland. There is no track as such, just a three-and-a-half-hour slog over the hills, climbing to almost 2000 feet on two occasions. Weaknesses are found out and regrets expressed about the beer and cigarettes enjoyed on the train during the journey northwards.

Back at Ardintigh the situation is not exactly a picnic on the lochside. When the boat pulls in towards the shore it has to be steadied by two men standing in several feet of water while the remainder carry the kit ashore. The cooks, or cook, are always included in the baggage party. They go ashore first and begin preparing the cook house for their first meal, supper, and a brew of tea for everyone when the party coming overland arrives. Often amazement is expressed by the new arrivals, not so much at the lack of facilities as at the way what facilities there are actually work. There is, after all, electricity when it begins to get dark in the evening, hot water in the showers and efficient lavatories.

The overland party have certainly shaken off any cobwebs remaining from the train journey northwards by the time they arrive. Twelve miles of hill, peat bog and crisp fresh air is a fine cure for a hangover. They are shown their billets, collect their packs from the foreshore and stow their gear. After a hot supper the whole party then assembles for a briefing on the camp, the surrounding area and the plans for the week ahead.

It is interesting for me, having made the introduction to Ardintigh, to step back and watch the faces of the men while either an officer or NCO continues with the briefing. Some simply sit staring in disbelief that they have managed to get themselves into such a situation while others show obvious excitement as the plans are revealed. We have never actually had a deserter, but that first evening would be the time to leave if some had a choice! More often than not, particularly if the weather is kind, spirits soon rise and men find their own level at coping with the tasks.

The cook is assigned one or two helpers on a daily rota while a similar roster assigns men to cleaning duties in the shower and toilet block, the accommodation and the camp area as a whole. After the long journey, the boat trip or the walk and a few cans of beer from the shop, most men are ready for an early night's sleep, only the sound of the wind blowing through the gaps in the stonework of the Cave, the breaking of waves on the beach and the occasional cry of a wild animal to disturb their well-earned rest. The officer and the NCOs sometimes come over to the house for a nightcap or a hot chocolate but often bed is the greatest attraction at Ardintigh on the first evening.

The next day's activities begin early. If the group has a piper, at my request, he goes down to the flag pole and plays reveille. I love the sound of the pipes, particularly when played at Ardintigh. 'The Dark Island' is one of my favourite pieces; it sounds nothing short of beautiful when played on the lochside on a summer evening. The cook brews tea and makes breakfast while khaki figures struggle in the dawn to the wash house. Breakfast over, the camp cleaned, the men parade to be divided into two groups, one to go canoeing, the other rock climbing and abseilling.

The canoeing group goes to the water's edge in olive green combat trousers and shirts carrying the canoes and paddles. Then they are told to walk out into the loch, swim 10 yards out and then swim parallel to the shore for as far as they can and come ashore. This is the essential swimming test. Before 1977 we made them swim out to a mark, round it and back, about 200 yards in all, but during a similar exercise at Aviemore, across the Highlands, two soldiers were drowned that year. Apparently one had been hit by cramp in the cold water and began to flounder. An instructor ashore, watching for just such an event, rushed into the water and swam strongly to the struggling man. The cold and exertion gave him cramp too. While the rest of the group watched helplessly from the beach both men sank from sight in the deep loch. Having read the report, I decided to keep the swimming activity in reach of the shallower water along the edge of the loch. Apart from keeping swimmers inshore I never allow men to go out on the water in canoes without a safety boat in attendance, my original workboat being put to this use. Once the swimming exercise is complete there are instructions on how to climb into the boat from the beach without capsizing it and training in capsizing and righting the canoes. Once reasonably confident in the basic skills of canoeing, the whole party makes its way to the far side of the loch if the weather allows or round to the shelter of Tarbert if not.

At Tarbert the other squad is learning the first steps of rock climbing on a sheer rock face of over 100 feet which rises out of the loch. Each man, roped up to another on the top of the cliff, makes his climb watched by the instructor. Once the whole squad has made at least one climb they abseille down the face at a fast but controlled speed.

After everyone has met at Ardintigh for lunch the two squads change sides, the canoeing party heading off round the loch for cliff climbing and the others tackling the canoes and swimming. If there are too many for two squads then a third squad is sent off on a navigational exercise up in the hills to the southwest of the centre. That evening, after drying their kit, they talk through the day and generally relax.

Every party usually spends two days and one night out in the hills. For this the men are divided into groups of four, each group often led by the least experienced man to give him confidence. The leaders are chosen by the NCOs who make their own way into the hills to provide contacts for the small teams as they progress from one grid reference to the next. The men usually cover about twenty-five miles a day. It may not seem a great distance, but in the hills of western Scotland it is enough for people with limited hill and mountain experience. As evening falls they make camp for the night, sleeping in what the army call a basher, a tent made from a poncho cape supported by sticks and held down by stones, and cook their meal on an open fire.

Teams of four are ideal. If one man should be injured, twisting an ankle or even breaking a leg, then the others can get him back to base, but even so it is quite a hike by boat to reach medical help. For real emergencies I have marked out a helicopter pad near the beach. Up to now I have not had to use this except for Cameron and some of his friends who, to save time, fly from the south to Glasgow and then charter a helicopter for the remaining journey north.

Success and failure in the hills depends on map reading.

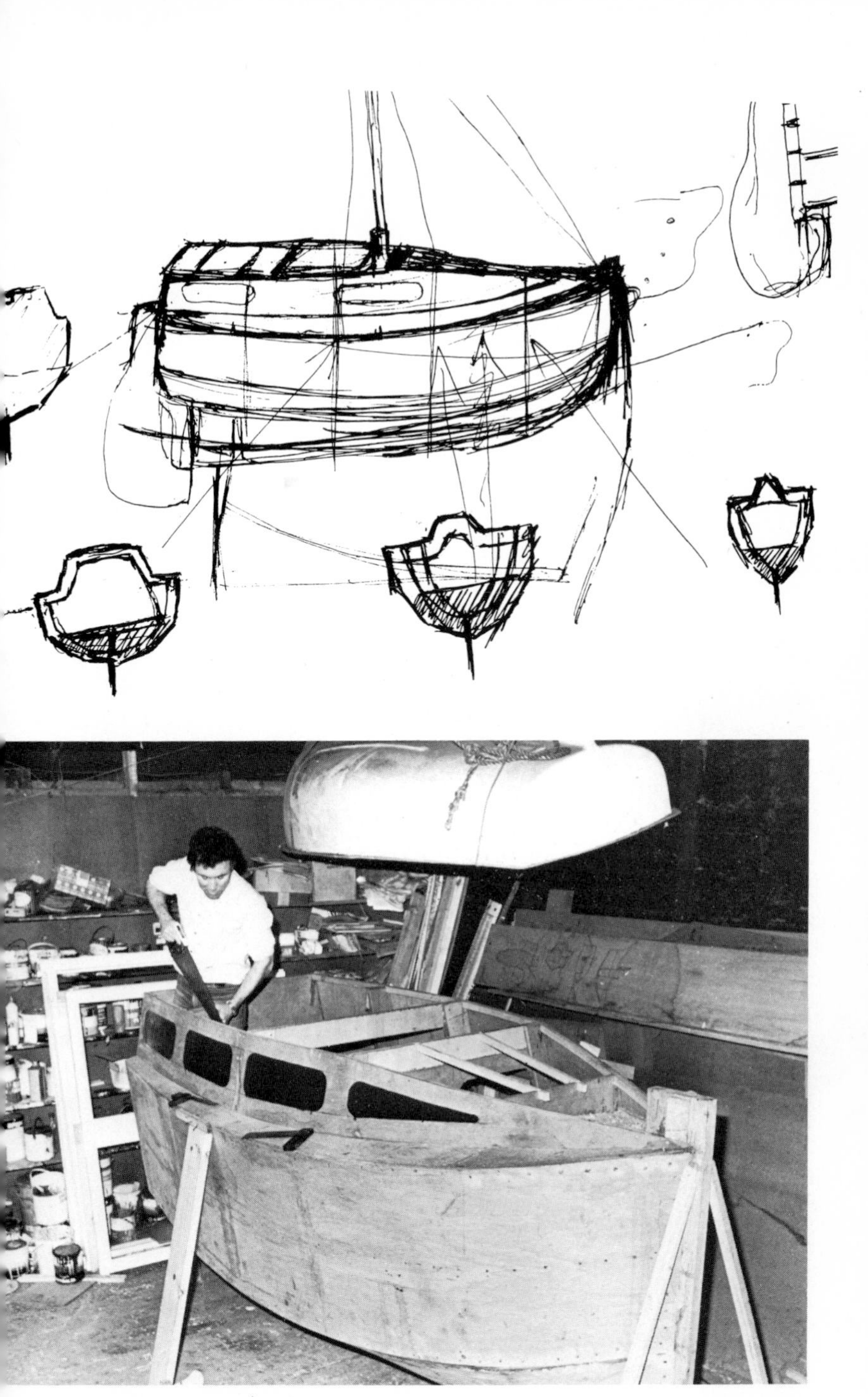

Top: The working 'plans' for *Giltspur*!

Above: Building the transatlantic bedroom

Lower away! Leaving the kipper factory workshop, Mallaig

Top: Jill launched the boat locally at Mallaig. Not all the champagne was wasted!

Above: *Giltspur* was launched again, by Claire Francis on the Thames at Windsor

Top: Anxious moments of farewell
Above: Loaded, waiting for the off

Nervous, posed, raring to go

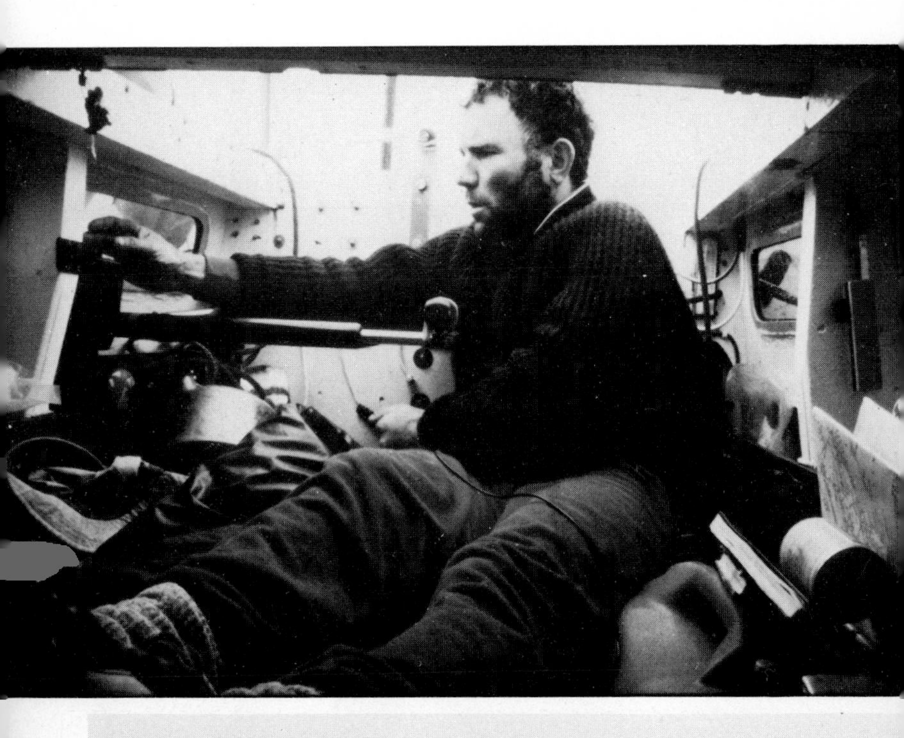

Top: My home – mid-Atlantic

Above: Chaos! Arrival at Falmouth, 12 August 1982

Top: Ah, well! Back to washing!

Above: The bit I left behind – Transatlantic II

Rule Britannia

This means learning to find the best route between various points, following contours around the edge of the hills rather than charging up and down the sides of steep mountains. It is easy to become lost in the hills, so careful and detailed briefing is a very important part of this particular exercise. I also insist that the soldiers who go into the hills carry more than they think they will need, particularly in the summer months when the temperature on the west coast can reach tropical proportions. We have had occasional scares when soldiers, particularly the younger ones, suffer from exposure. This is caused by a lowering of body temperature, often due to a cool wind blowing through wet clothing when physical activity has slowed down. It works both ways. If physical activity slows, then the circulation also slows and the body cools. As the body cools, then it becomes harder to keep moving and general apathy and inertia set in, leading to unconsciousness and eventually death.

If a man, or even the occasional woman from one of the Women's Royal Army Corps groups, begins to show signs of exposure, then the remedy is clearly pointed out in their instructions. The casualty is stripped of wet clothing and wrapped in blankets or put in a sleeping bag. Another person gets into the sleeping bag or blankets with the casualty, the contact of body heat being one of the best methods of bringing the sufferer back to normal temperature. Help is sought from Ardintigh or any nearby croft or homestead and the casualty taken indoors and put into a warm dry bed as soon as possible, again the system of body contact being used – nice if you happen to be with a group of WRACs, though at this stage the victim is past caring who is sharing the bed and sleeping bag. Hot drinks, but never alcohol, are given and conversation kept up if the casualty is conscious. Never must a sufferer from exposure be allowed to lapse into coma.

Constant talking, cajoling, even bullying, is maintained if a casualty has been brought into the warmth of the house to be nursed by Jill and one or two colleagues working in shifts. Once the sufferer has recovered enough to move about again, he is given small tasks to help him maintain the build up of interest in recovery.

After two nights on the hills the men return to the centre to prepare for the next day's activity which can vary from a full day's canoe trip to the head of the loch where they make bonfires from driftwood, watch wild life and swim from the beach, to climbing my favourite mountain, Sgùrr-na-Ciche.

On the final night at Ardintigh there is usually a football match followed by a barbecue round a bonfire on the beach, with beer and a sing-song. Sometimes this party becomes rowdier than I personally enjoy, but usually it is a good evening.

An early start next morning; the camp area is given a final clean and inspection, the boat loaded with kit and the long walk back to Mallaig and the train journey south begins. It has always amused me to see the difference between the men who had walked into Ardintigh a week earlier and those who walk out. They look fitter, have a spring in their step and a sense of achievement seems to prevail. Many promise to come back and, service commitments allowing, many do.

Now, back at Mallaig, it is their turn to pull the legs of the next batch arriving at the station and peace descends on Ardintigh for a few hours until the new arrivals come in over the hill.

12 A Rut?

With the increasing amount of kit and stores that the army were bringing to Ardintigh, *Sea Otter* was no longer big enough. While in Mull I had seen some good-looking steel working boats, ideal in size for what I needed. They were called Samson Stormmasters and were built at Market Harborough by a firm called Springers. I went south to the yard to see the boats, which were built on a canal. I liked what I saw: they were good and solid, with a wide beam, proper accommodation in a two-berth cabin, a wheelhouse above, a galley area and a marine toilet. They were, for me, expensive, about £12,000, but I was making money so I placed an order for one to be built, adding a few specifications of my own. The boat was 31 feet long, 11 feet wide and weighed almost ten tons. Most boats have a beam of about one third the total length, but the Stormmaster exceeded this – a good load carrier, that was certain. She also had a double keel so I could beach her safely at Ardintigh while unloading and loading stores.

It took the yard four months to build the boat, which was then put aboard a low-loading road trailer and towed to Fort William. There were no cranes at Mallaig big enough to lift her into the harbour, so Fort William and a sea trip from there was the only answer. In any case, the road from Fort William over the hills to Mallaig, single-track with passing places, was, in the opinion of the police escorting the load, too narrow. Full of excitement Jill and I went to Fort William with her father, Wanda, one of Jill's girlfriends, and an army officer who, with a couple of soldiers, had offered to help.

The plan was to lift the boat into the water and take her down Loch Linnhe, through the Sound of Mull, past Tobermory and northwards past the Point of Ardnamurchan and across the Sound of Arisaig to Mallaig and home. It sounded easy, but all the best laid plans are, in Scotland, occasionally capable of falling apart.

We reached Fort William but the boat was not there. It eventually arrived later that day after the crane had been locked away in a compound for the night. I gave the crane driver £5 and it was magically released. It was then, after the crane had arrived at the canal basin at Corpach, on the edge of Loch Eil, that the crane driver announced that the crane could not lift the boat, it was not big enough; the ten-ton boat would stretch it to danger point.

'Stretch it, then,' I said, passing over another £5. Taking plenty of time, the boat was lifted from the trailer and inched to the water's edge. At last she was in the water and the crew embarked. We checked the engine, fuel and emergency equipment, taking on several jerry cans of diesel oil. We launched her with champagne, naming her *Gypsy Rover* and after decking her out with streamers and balloons, we set sail down Loch Linnhe. The loch was calm and beautiful as we cruised southwest, but I decided to drop anchor for the night rather than try night navigation in strange waters and a strange boat. The wind was beginning to increase so it seemed a wise decision.

Next morning I had a struggle to start the motor, but it turned out that the battery terminals were loose. After tightening them, we were away once more, into the Sound of Mull towards Tobermory.

At Tobermory the wind increased and the forecast was bad for rounding Ardnamurchan, the most westerly point on the British mainland. I asked the coastguards what they thought. They advised us to stay until the weather moderated, but the army officer was anxious to get back to his men at Ardintigh. He had his turn with the coastguards and persuaded them that it was, after all, safe to sail. Right,

I thought, we'll go and you can see just how bad bad can be.

Jill's father, George, being ex-Royal Navy, had other ideas. No way was he going round Ardnamurchan in a new boat in that weather, so he went ashore and headed for Mallaig via the various island ferries. We sailed. Hardly were we out of harbour than the officer began being seasick; he was very quiet and in a bad way. We rounded the point through rough steep seas, passed by the big ferry which slowed to see if we were all right. We were rolling like a pig, so I changed course for the Isle of Muck. The seas, by now, were gigantic and it was all I could do to keep her on a straight course; the wheel was situated fairly high and I had to stand on an ammunition box to see out. One big wave threw me backwards and broke the cabin door right off its hinges; it nearly went overboard. I couldn't leave the wheel for a second and the girls were mopping the sweat from my face.

I headed for Muck, going slowly and taking five long hours for the last eight miles. Everyone on board apart from myself was far from well. Then we hit another snag. Steam began to pour from the engine compartment. I lifted the hatch and found the engine swamped with water which was about one third of the way up the crankcase. I was already furious with the officer for persuading me to go to sea against my better judgement and as furious with myself for being persuaded.

'Right!' I shouted at him. 'You can bloody well get down there and start pumping!' He set to with a will, driven by fear, I am sure, of sinking. So hard did he pump that he pulled the head off the pump.

'Get the electric pump,' I shouted over the howling wind. 'Hold the end in the bilges and run it until the boat's dry!'

Green in the face, he struggled to lower the end of the pump into the deepest part of the hull and we were soon dry. The water had come through the hatches which were fine for canals but no good in those waters. (When safely home I altered them by remaking them with deep sills round the rubber seals.) We took soundings going into the small harbour at Muck and everyone began to recover as we anchored for the night. The Tobermory coastguards, whom I telephoned from Muck, were pleased to receive the call and learn that we had arrived in one piece.

Next morning the weather had moderated and we set out for Ardintigh, arriving safely, though there was a certain atmosphere between myself and the young officer. I was not sorry when he set off for the south, but the experience had taught me a lesson. Make a decision and stick to it, whatever persuasive forces are at work.

Gypsy Rover turned out to be superb for diving and load carrying, so I beached *Sea Otter* for a new coat of paint and a refit before trying to sell her and used *Gypsy Rover* for the day-to-day chores.

One of the regular tasks was to restock the camp from the cash-and-carry at Inverness, the nearest such place to Mallaig, a round trip of 250 miles. Every three or four weeks during the summer months I would drive over, taking the back road via Aviemore and call to see some friends, Mr and Mrs Utsi, at the Reindeer Park. He was a Finn who had met his wife while she was on a study of Finland from Cambridge University. They had brought reindeer back to Scotland and established a breeding herd in the central Highlands which has become both a worthwhile experiment and a tourist attraction. I felt close to them and their way of life, living in the wilds and close to nature.

I had known them before I met Jill. When they heard that I was to be married they were among the first to send congratulations. He reckoned that marriage would be the making of me. He was right, not only in my opinion but in that of others in Scotland and elsewhere who knew me both before and after Jill joined me at Ardintigh.

The Inverness trips were a welcome break for Jill and me, perhaps more so for Jill who, although perfectly happy at Ardintigh, sometimes missed the accepted conveniences of ordinary modern life. One such facility was the telephone, not just to enable her to talk to her friends, but to make the whole running of the camp so much simpler and more efficient.

I often wondered just how many bookings I might have lost in those early years simply because it took so long for letters and telegrams to reach us. The mail boat, *Western Isles*, came up to Tarbert twice a week weather permitting, on Mondays and Fridays. A telegram or letter arriving at Mallaig post office on Monday would take another five days to reach me unless I went into town by boat during the week. There had to be a better way, so I wrote to the Post Office asking for them to look into the possibility of providing a telephone link to the camp, perhaps via Inverie where there was already a relay.

Back came their quotation. They would build a relay station at Inverie and another at Ardintigh. Cost? £6000 for the installation and a rental of £3000 per year. It would have been, surely, one of the most expensive telephones in the world. The £6000 was perhaps reasonable for a system that would last forty or fifty years, but the rental, £60 per week, would have been crippling, so the idea was shelved.

I got in touch with the Member of Parliament for Inverness-shire, Russell Johnston, but even he could do little to help. The GPO had put their side of the problem and I reckoned at the time that they had simply priced me out of the market by imposing a high rental to deter me from going ahead. Later, much later, the new radio-telephone link system arrived in the communications marketplace and we now, today, have a radio link telephone.

Jill and I invented our own signalling system so that once I was on the way to Mallaig by boat she could call me back if some emergency occurred. She would get a double sheet and hang it out of an upstairs window so that it was stretched across the gables to the next window. If I saw this signal, I would turn back, but it was a primitive method. It only worked as long as I was still in sight of the camp. It did save me a few wasted journeys, however, when I had set off to Mallaig to collect soldiers or visitors and they meanwhile had arrived over the hills by foot.

Apart from the sheer inconvenience, the delays over telegrams and mail were not really as bad as they seem. When the mail arrived at Donald and Jessie's post office at Tarbert I would either walk over the hill or canoe round the point to collect it, stopping for a cup of tea and a chat. It was contact with other people and something that both they and I enjoyed. To have a telegram delivered was another matter. For the mail boat to bring it from Mallaig by special delivery cost me up to £60, for a message which cost about £4 to send. That situation still prevails today, though telegrams now are a thing of the past and more and more messages arrive via the radio super phone.

Our early lack of telephone contact with the outside world may, sadly, have cost a man his life. A helicopter was flying out over the loch from Inverie when people there thought they saw it drop towards the water. It was closer to my side of the loch when it fell. We knew nothing of the trouble until next day. One of the crew had made it to the shore but the other had drowned. If the people at Inverie had been able to contact us, we might have managed to rescue him with one of our boats.

Helicopters were becoming more and more frequent in the Highlands in the late 1970s. The army occasionally sent one up to Ardintigh to make the recce trip, and we would be given the odd ride around the loch. Once we went to the top of Sgùrr-na-Ciche and another time to the mine across the loch where, during the last world war, mica had been discovered, the only source of this material, which was used in the insulation of radio and other electrical equipment. A track still goes up to the disused mine, a feat of strength and ingenuity that still amazes me.

In order to crack the rock on the top of the steep-sided mountain the miners needed a compressor to work the drills and power hammers. There was only a rough track to the site, so they took the heavy machinery across the loch from Mallaig, unloaded it on the shore and then pulled it up the hillside using blocks and tackles. It took them almost three weeks to inch the equipment to the top before the mining of the precious wafer-thin material could begin. During army visits we would take the men across the loch from Ardintigh to the same piece of rough shoreline and let them climb to the mine where, even to this day, people come and hunt for a type of amethyst which can still occasionally be found among the remains of the mica workings.

One of the occasional bonuses that the army brought to Ardintigh was the cinema. A group will sometimes import a projector and one or two feature films to be shown in the evenings. Once the army have finished with them, we take the films, complete with the projector, to the estate club at

Inverie and show them there the next day. There is always a full turnout for these film evenings, which often develops into a social occasion with beer and cold food being provided by the people from the estate.

Late in 1978 I managed to sell *Sea Otter*, my old and faithful workboat, to a fisherman on the island of Iona. She had cost me £1600 but I had looked after her well. Boats are like property. If you look after them they appreciate in value. *Sea Otter* was forty-eight years old when I sold her, for £3000. It was not an inflated price, but simply reflected how the cost of living had risen since I had bought her six years earlier. Now *Sea Otter*, the centre of so much that had happened at Ardintigh, was off to a further life of work, to be used for fishing and diving for scallops by her new owner.

From 1976 to 1979 life continued at Ardintigh in a pattern of its own. I continued to dive for clams, maintain the buildings and make trips to Mallaig and further afield.

One night, when coming back from Mallaig in the launch, I was almost run down by an apparently unmanned east-coast Scottish fishing boat. I was well up into the loch when I met her. Missing me by a few feet, she steamed on towards the shore. I opened up my engine and caught her up, flashing my lights and blowing the horn. Suddenly lights appeared on her deck, much swearing followed, the engine roared and she began to slow and move astern away from the rocks. She stopped again, went slowly ahead, turned and sped back out to sea. To this day I have no idea what she was doing steaming around at night, unlit and heading for a rocky shore.

About this time Russian and Polish fish factory ships began to appear in Loch Nevis, anchoring well above Ardintigh. Fishing boats from all around Britain followed the mackerel shoals round the coast, selling their catch to the Eastern Europeans rather than to the home market. We saw little of the crews, though once in a while they would give a wave as we passed. They only went ashore a couple of times a week for a few hours' shopping in Mallaig. I never saw them ashore on the loch, although they may have landed for the occasional walk on the lochside because one of the soldiers reported that he had found a Russian flag flying on a small hillock at the head of the loch. Since the fish have dwindled, the factory ships have not been back for several years. However, although the fishing has declined, I feel that Mallaig will survive once the oil business moves down to the west coast of Scotland, though it will probably be a few years before this happens.

During the summer the factory ships first appeared, Cameron Mackintosh and his friends came back to the loch in a miniature hovercraft which caused something of a sensation in Mallaig. I could not wait to get my hands on her, but my skill as a hovercraft pilot was short-lived. I tore around the loch at 50 knots before burning a hole in my shirt and back on the engine. I then rushed up the beach in the amazing machine and collided with the rescue boat which was beached on the grass, hitting the stern and tearing out the transom. That was enough of hovercraft for me, I decided, as I looked for the tools to knock the dents out of the hovercraft and make repairs to the extensive damage I had inflicted on the boat.

Apart from the groups who came for the adventure training we had an amazing number of visitors during the summer months. In 1978 and 1979 there were about 150 people who signed our visitor's book. Most of them would stay at least one night. They varied from people like David Stirling, founder of the SAS, and other army friends, to Auntie Kay from Ireland and Jill's family. One day I had the surprise of my life. I was working in the camp when, suddenly, round the headland appeared three people riding pushbikes towards me across the grass. That was a first at Ardintigh, if ever there was one. I dropped my paint brush and stared in disbelief. To reach Ardintigh by bicycle means covering miles of rough tracks followed by several long steep climbs over the hills.

The cyclists were three Yorkshiremen who had ridden from Yorkshire to Fort William and then taken the rough route through the glens and hills, sometimes carrying the bikes for three or four miles at a time. We had a friendly chat and I gave them tea and some beer.

For about two years I had been suggesting to Archie Lawrie and his friends in the Mallaig Moto-Cross club that they should try the ride out on their motorbikes to Ardintigh, using the track along Loch Morar and then the steep hill path behind the camp. Beer would be waiting. While I was talking to the intrepid Yorkshire trio the air was rent with the roar of engines and several members of the club appeared, for a few moments very pleased with themselves – until they saw the pushbikes. At first they assumed that the bikes had been brought up the loch by boat, but when they heard that they had been ridden and carried over the hills from Fort William their sense of achievement was a little deflated.

Everyone sat on the grass enjoying the summer sun and the beer. Then it was time to go, the motorbikes roaring off back over the hill while the pedal cyclists set off down the rough shore of the loch to Mallaig.

It has always amazed me that one can spend weeks at Ardintigh and see no one, then suddenly the place is like the middle of a town on market day with people milling around everywhere, but of all those occasions when the world arrived, the day of the cyclists is one I shall never forget.

The problems, the challenge and the wild attractiveness of Ardintigh instills a sense of being which is different from that which is accepted as normal elsewhere. Religion, if by that word one means Christianity, has never really meant a great deal to me. I still remember the religious instruction, church services and other teaching that was forced upon me at the orphanage. I think, subconsciously, I connect any religious feelings I might have with those days and, grateful though I am for much of it when I look back, like the life at the orphanage, I left it behind once I was out in the world.

When in the army I used to go to compulsory church services but today I do not get any really deep feelings when I go into a church. If there is a carol service or Sunday evening church service on television I enjoy watching, remembering the better times at the orphanage. If one looks at all the alternative religions in the world, they are offering basically the same thing, a code by which to live with other people. I cannot believe, for one minute, that because I have been taught the Christian religion, I am any better than someone who believes in something different.

As for some sort of life after this one, well, I find the idea hard to believe and rarely give it a second thought. I am too busy sorting out this life to think of something ahead which I cannot understand. Here I am and here I get on with it. I often wonder what happened before the religions which we accept or are taught today existed. The Romans and Greeks had their gods; the Pacific islanders worshipped the sun. One cannot blame them for that: the sun was the great source of power, fire, heat and growth; it was there every day and was a crucial influence on life.

In most humans there is a need to believe in some power greater than themselves. I can understand that; I believe that there is some such power, but I cannot identify it. Many people, after a week of work and worry of modern life, put on their best clothes and go to church for a sort of spiritual cleansing. It does them good, makes them feel happier. Just as they go to church, I go out for a ten- or fifteen-mile walk over the hills, thinking over the past week, planning the next one. That is my cleansing.

Everyone is entitled to his own view of religion. I can see no reason, if one believes in something strongly enough, why one should not start one's own religion so long as it makes people live together in harmony and friendliness. I have been asked how I felt about God, whatever, when out in the ocean or in the jungle. As I have said, I am sure there is some sort of overall power, and I prayed to him at times, but when it comes down to it it is up to the individual to get on with it. No god is going to mend a broken mast, a torn sail or prevent an ambush.

Perhaps my religion is based on patriotism. I am a great patriot, flying the national flag from my home and boats with pride. Patriotism can almost be a religion if one believes in one's country enough and I reckon that Britain is the finest country on earth when it comes to attitudes to life. Certainly there is rather too much red restrictive tape around sometimes, but at Ardintigh we only suffer from a minimum of what is simply the wheels of law and order becoming clogged by too many people trying to drive them.

I seldom become depressed on my own account; however, when I watch the television or read a newspaper, often a week old by the time it reaches Ardintigh, I feel concern about the way some things in life are going. As I set out on a day of diving for clams, fishing for lobster, painting the sheds or collecting soldiers from Mallaig, I feel sorry for the people setting off for a day in a factory facing a job like the one I had chopping legs off chickens as they went past on a conveyor belt. Every day is one more day of living one's life. One does not get that day again, so the very best must be made of it. If nothing else, my children will never have to work like that, will never know the basic sadness and the fight for survival in an orphanage; they will learn to survive in open countryside and appreciate the real values of life. Ardintigh and I, combined, will surely see to that.

The problems of young people today bother me and I see something of them at Ardintigh; we have boys from approved schools and other places who really have no appreciation of anything except a stereo headset and the occasional punch-up. A period of community service might help them. Not planting trees or digging council parks and gardens, but building homes for old people, right from scratch, or improving existing housing – something where they can see the result at the end of the day.

Leadership is important, a point borne out at Ardintigh over and over again. If a group of soldiers arrives with a good officer and NCOs who really keep them at it with plenty of activity then the soldiers always seem to enjoy their stay. On the other hand, if there is no real organization, then after a week they cannot wait for the march over the hills back to the train or transport at Mallaig. It is the same with the kids in civilian life. Given the right leadership, they can achieve something, and that leadership must start at a young age with the parents. In my own case, one must read 'orphanage and army' for 'parents' and it was the army that did most of the good work because the orphanage, with every good will in the world, taught me survival, not compatibility.

Ardintigh also taught me a great deal about myself. I had learned a lot in the army, particularly in the jungle and desert, but it was in Scotland, living month in, month out, up on the lonely lochside, completely cut off and alone, where I really discovered myself. I enjoyed the life, enjoyed my own company, and survived. To do this one either has to be mad or completely at one with oneself and one's circumstances. When I married Jill the adjustments we each had to make, her to Ardintigh and me to marriage and permanent company, was a two-way effort.

Now I have my home, family and responsibility, but one of my basic philosophies, probably formed in the days of the orphanage, is that the more one has, the more one has to worry about. I said as much to John Ridgway when I was visiting his adventure school at Ardmore which he was expanding into quite an empire. He employs resident instructors, has a fleet of boats and his territory covers a large area. He threw my own thoughts back at me over my transatlantic sailing trip which was beginning to develop in my mind.

I suppose the next tingling of itchy feet began in 1979. I used to enjoy watching documentaries on the television about faraway places, was frustrated that my Antarctic and Everest plans had come to nothing and was subconsciously turning over various ideas for an adventure. Life was a little restricting, even though I was living in the wilds, the evening trips across to the estate club at Inverie with some of the soldiers being the main social highlight.

But in May 1980, our first child, James, was born. I decided that it would be best for Jill to be with her family in Yorkshire for the birth. Ardintigh in winter was too remote, although we probably could have coped. I have seen births in the kampongs, the long houses, in Borneo, but in the western world childbirth is a different business from that in the Far East jungles. There the women simply get on with it, the whole process taking about twenty minutes from start to finish. In the west women seem to do a great deal more huffing and puffing. I was at the birth, a fine boy, James, weighing in at just over 9 lb, a big baby. Once Jill was ready we headed back to Ardintigh, the baby causing quite a stir among our friends in Mallaig and Inverie.

13 Striking Back for Britain

During the early summer of 1981, with James seeming to grow bigger every day, a photograph arrived from America, sent by the American yachtsman Gerry Speiss who, a couple of years before, had crossed the Atlantic in *Yankee Girl*, a boat only 10 feet long. It set me thinking. The new Atlantic records to be broken were either for the fastest crossing single-handed in a boat of any length, or in a fully manned sailing boat of unlimited size or, the record which appealed to me, a crossing in the smallest boat, regardless of time. Size was the crucial factor.

Next year, 1982, was to be National Maritime Year. What a year to break a new sailing record for Britain. I had the picture of Gerry's boat and from this I drew rough sketches of a plan for a boat. I wanted to discuss the project with one or two friends, so I went across the Highlands to Findhorn to see Donald Davidson. He was very direct. He listened to my ideas and then asked me why I did not get moving and do it. It was all I needed to start me on the long path that, a full year later, led to my putting to sea from the coast of Newfoundland. Donald told me that I would need an agent to help me find sponsors for the voyage and introduced me to John Young. He, in turn, said that he would try to find a major sponsor; I meanwhile would look for other backers prepared to supply the necessary equipment, ranging from timber for building the boat to food during the trip. We went to see a Glasgow-based newspaper, but they politely turned my idea down.

After a lot of trouble Trevor Moore managed to get a copy of Gerry Speiss's book about his crossing in *Yankee Girl* and from this I copied the plan of his boat. This would be the basis of the boat that I planned to build. I took my plans to a naval architect in Glasgow who specialized in designing yachts and small boats. He was very interested and helpful and confirmed that such a boat could be built to cross the Atlantic if sailed by the right person. It would cost about £10,000 to design and build; even then, in 1981, a boat cost a basic £1000 per foot length. £10,000! That was about twice my budget for the whole trip, including building the boat, shipping it to Canada and the crossing itself, not to mention stores and accommodation at either end of the trip. I went back to Ardintigh to think. It looked as though I would have to build the boat myself.

Not too disheartened, I carried on with my own plans, but the news from my agent, John Young, was not good. He was not having much luck in finding a backer in a time of economic recession. I decided to end the arrangement with John and find a backer for myself. Meanwhile suppliers in Inverness and Fort William very kindly gave me timber for the framework and plywood to cover the hull. I gathered the materials together in Mallaig. The Smith brothers, Hamish and Ian, were good enough to let me use their workshop which had once been used to smoke kippers when the herring fishing was at its height.

I had told Jill of my plan but she was not too enthusiastic. She seemed to think that it was just another hare-brained scheme which would eventually fold up and disappear. She was expecting our second child at Christmas 1981 and, as before, went to Yorkshire for the birth. I moved from Ardintigh to the caravan at Morar to organize the start of building the boat and keep in touch with Jill. When the time came for the baby to be born I joined her in Yorkshire for a week. The baby, Ryan, was fine and so was Jill. While awaiting the birth, she had written to a hundred or more top companies, sending them a special brochure that we had produced called

'Atlantic Adventure' which outlined the voyage and gave details of my past.

We also contacted the *Mary Rose* Trust in the hope that they might sponsor me or that I might be able to make the crossing into a fund-raising trip for them, calling the boat *Mary Rose II* and promoting the sponsored sail in every post office in Britain. By doing this I reckoned that we could easily raise £1 million for the Trust and, at the same time, pay for the voyage. They were very encouraging and enthusiastic. I met Ian Dahl from the Trust. He agreed that we could raise a considerable sum but he had to take the scheme to his committee. Committees! Here we go again, just like the Antarctic and Everest trips, bound by red tape. I kept calling him, but he seemed to be getting no nearer a decision. However, Donald Davidson was urging me on, while the Fun People, particularly Trevor Moore and Phil Rhodes, were looking for help in the south.

Trevor, along with Jill, suggested that the answer was to go to London to the 1982 Boat Show and look for possible sponsors in the marine trade. The boat was now half finished, the keel laid, the sides planked and the compartments built into the compact little hull.

The replies came back from the many companies to which Jill had written asking for help. All said much the same. The economic recession meant that they were short of cash for this sort of project but they wished me luck. So it was back to building, helped by a local carpentry apprentice, Douglas Fairbairn, when he had time to spare. Another friend, Rod Wood, from Dalkeith, also came up whenever he had time and helped in the construction. We covered the hull with Cascover sheathing, making it doubly strong. The Thames marine ply would probably have been tough enough on its own, but I had to be sure; in fact the hull never let in a drop of water through the planking.

The mast, sails, self-steering gear, radios and the other accessories would have to be found at the Boat Show. I worked away in the winter cold, hoping that the visit to London was going to be successful, particularly after the setbacks with the approaches made to British industry generally. It was apparent that the most expensive cost in building a boat as small as this was the labour, so by doing most of the work myself I was saving a relative fortune.

Jill was warming to the idea of the trip now that she realized I meant business. It was time that I explained to her in full my reasons for wanting to do it, and this I did one evening in the caravan. I explained my thoughts as best I could, how I felt that I must do at least one more thing of my own before settling down to the life that I had learned to accept and enjoy so much. It might seem irresponsible, but, as always, I had considered the risks and ways of overcoming them.

'Listen, love,' I said, as we sat at home, a howling Atlantic gale lashing the caravan, 'I don't want the kids to grow up and say that their Dad rowed the Atlantic alone in seventy days and would have won the record for the smallest sailing boat, but he met and married Mum! I want them to say that I did it *because* I married you!'

She seemed impressed for a moment, but didn't say much. It was a bit like the meeting with Colonel John Slim, the CO of the SAS, before I rowed the Atlantic. She was, after all, the CO now! I'm not sure what I would have done if she had said a definite no, but it was a situation I had to face. She smiled, a tear in sight, and said quietly, 'Tom, I couldn't stop you if I wanted to, so I might as well get used to the idea and help! I can't even go off and have a baby without you starting something daft, but then I should have realized that when I married you. Perhaps that's why I did.'

We laughed together and had a warm family evening as the wind howled outside.

We packed the car for the journey south to the Boat Show, dropping the children off with Jill's family in Yorkshire. We were full of optimism when we reached London and the welcome which awaited us at Cameron's flat. Next morning we set off for Earl's Court. We showed our shopping list to various manufacturers and soon had some useful promises of help, but I still needed a principal sponsor.

Then, on about the fourth day of our London visit we hit the jackpot, or at least heard that our financial worries might be solved. David Stride, one of the Fun People, supplied packaging equipment to the army and through this work knew Ted Redicliffe, a director of the Giltspur organization, itself part of the Unigate group of companies. They were considering sponsoring the trip. Discussions followed during the next month while, back in Scotland, I continued working on the boat.

She was looking very good. Strong, deep for her length, and with enough space below the small deck to take the many things I would need to carry, over and above food for a hundred days, if I was to survive any unexpected problem or disaster that might befall me. Kit began arriving from the manufacturers who had offered help. There was a life raft, flares, a radio, a compass, paint, coils of rope and wire rigging, sails . . . even the mast.

I finished the building and rigging in early March and went back to the head offices of Giltspur near Windsor bridge where I met Ted Harker, the chief executive of the company. We got along from the start but we were still discussing plans rather than finance. I could not yet be absolutely certain I could go.

The launching at Mallaig was quite a party. Most of the town turned out, many of them more amused than impressed. Some, for fun, wrote suggestions for names on the boat: *Thy Kingdom Come, Moby's Ark.* We lowered her into the water with a crane from Ian and Hamish Smith's workshop in the old kipper factory, using a lorry for the short hop from the shed to the harbour side. Jill stood by with a bottle of champagne which she cracked on the bow. Down went the boat. Rod Wood was hidden aboard with a mass of small concrete blocks for ballast. The boat floated high, so we added more blocks while all the locals had a good look at her.

Then we took her up the loch to Ardintigh for final fitting-out and rigging before sea trials. David Cork, from Giltspur, came up to help and suggested that we fit a heavier deeper keel to the bottom of the oak keel, but this could be done later, before I set out. She already had half a ton of internal ballast. Her trials were partly for the benefit of the Fun People, who pulled her over by the mast to see what would happen when they let go. I need not have worried. The boat sprang back with such a flip that I banged my head as I sat below in the tiny cabin. Trials complete, we were ready to go.

In April, after more than two long months of waiting, I had news from London. Giltspur would help to underwrite the cost of the trip and top up my stretched finances. We were off. The launching ceremony, to be performed by Clare Francis, was to be held at Windsor during early May and the boat then prepared for shipment to Canada. There was a great deal to be said for having a sponsor like Giltspur. They ran a fleet of removal lorries, could pack stores in sealed plastic bags, handle shipping without even thinking about it, and several of the directors, living near the Solent, knew about sailing and the problems I was having to sort out.

Meanwhile I had been in touch with the people at the *Sunday Express* who had taken me on before for the rowing trip. Peter Vane was now foreign editor, based in London, so instead I met Jimmy Kinlay, the man in charge of features. My voyage was discussed with Sir John Junor, the editor, and a deal agreed. They would pay me an advance for my exclusive story when I reached Europe, the rest, the other half of the agreed sum, when I arrived. My impression of the *Sunday Express*, apart from the friendliness of the people I met there, was that it was run entirely by Scotsmen . . . no bad thing. Us Celts must stick together!

The launching day was a great success. The bridge from Windsor to Eton was a mass of people as *Giltspur*, as the boat was named, was lowered into the water after Clare had smashed a bottle of champagne over the little bow. Some people were openly critical, but no one actually said that I would not survive. Just as well!

I took Clare out on the Thames for a motor-sail, the outboard whirring away. It was apparent to some of the experts ashore that more stability was needed even though the stores were yet to be put aboard. This was a valid criticism, so Ted Redicliffe made arrangements for the boat to be taken to their Totton packaging works where a large slab of iron was bolted onto the bottom of the existing keel. We carried out trials in the confines of Southampton Water and the improvement was very noticeable. I never thought that *Giltspur* would roll right over, but we had managed to decrease the angle to which she would tilt.

It might have seemed to the expert yachtsman, the person who races his immaculate yacht on the Solent each weekend, a dramatic yet amateur measure, but *Giltspur* was a far cry from that type of boat. She was smaller in length than the average dinghy, yet designed for the fearsome Atlantic. She was built like a miniature tank. For the benefit of the expert, she sailed only off the wind, 90° to it on either tack being the best she could do. She was a downhill boat, built (one can hardly be impertinent enough to use the word 'designed') to sail across the Atlantic with the prevailing winds, winds from the west. A wind from any point east would mean either choosing the northern or southern tack, whichever gave the most easterly track. If the wind blew from the northeast, then I would sail southeast; if from the southeast, then, with luck, northeast. Only a dead-header, a gale from due east, would really stuff me . . . and it did.

Giltspur was taken to Liverpool and loaded onto a cargo ship for Canada. The stores had been packed in their many carefully labelled plastic bags and put in boxes. The old pre-para-jump butterflies were returning. Jill was obviously apprehensive but tried hard not to show it. She had spent days helping with all the office work that is now part of the preparation for any adventure. Whatever one escapes from by going to sea, the system makes up for it before and afterwards.

I decided that it would be easier for Jill if we said our goodbyes in Scotland. I hate departures at the best of times, but this was really the first time I had ever left anyone whom I could really call family. Sure, I had made trips into the hills, down to the south and about the country, but nothing like this. I made my last moments with Jill as quick as possible, gritted my teeth and headed for the station. I must have made an odd sight among the holidaymakers in their sunshine gear and the businessmen in their suits. There I was in deckboots, jeans, sailing anorak, carrying a sailbag containing my overnight gear.

From then on, until I sailed from St John's, it was a case of having been there before. My mind kept going back from thoughts of Jill and the kids to my last voyage in 1969. Below, as the airliner headed west, I caught glimpses of the Atlantic, a grey wasteland flecked with white wave crests. I tried to sleep, but kept thinking of the task ahead. I must have stared down at the ocean for hours.

14 The Atlantic Again

I reached St John's to find that news of my plan had arrived before me but the boat had not. I was a mixed heap of anger, disappointment and frustration. Wondering what to do next, I paced around the hall outside the telephone booth at the airport from where I had called the agents for the shippers. I sat down and flipped through the pages of the local telephone directory to see whether the Squires family were still in St John's. After trying three numbers, I managed to track them down, but could not get through, so I decided to take a taxi.

Harold had obviously progressed up the local government tree and was living in an attractive house with a large garden. He and Jean were out when I arrived, but the children (they will not forgive me for that), now grown up, were very happy to see me. Elizabeth sat me down in the living room and we waited. When Harold and Jean returned, Jean walked into the room and looked around. She saw me, stared, with a look of blank surprise on her face as she searched for the stranger's name. Then it clicked.

'Tom!' she yelled. 'What a wonderful surprise!'

It was like coming home. We sat talking, catching up on news. I told them about Jill and the family, the adventure camp and the many things that had happened during the past twelve years. Then we discussed the problems of the boat. How long would it be before it showed up?

I stayed with the Squires, waiting. I dug their garden, went for runs and tried to keep busy. At last, after nine days, the boat arrived together with the crate of stores. Everything was unloaded, quickly cleared by the Canadian customs, and I could begin packing the stores, almost a ton, into the boat.

As before, I had many helpers in Canada, not least the Squires. We packed and repacked the plastic-sealed packets into every available space, rigged the mast, stowed and hanked on sails, secured the cooker and small outboard engine that would double as generator, and attached the self-steering vane and the wind-driven battery charger. News was filtering through that an American, Bill Dunlop, had sailed from Maine in the States in his tiny boat *Wind's Will*, 8 inches shorter than *Giltspur*. Good luck to him, I thought, and meant it.

At last, after almost three days of work, preparation and checking, I was ready – but the weather was not. A screaming gale, straight out of the Arctic, swept the harbour. There was no question of sailing, the direction of the wind and the coastal dangers off St John's making the risks too great. I waited one more frustrating day. The wind moderated, giving me an offshore push next day, so with friends, the press and many wellwishers watching, I clambered into the tiny cockpit, hoisted the mainsail and jib, started the outboard and made my way out into the harbour. Spectator boats stayed with me as I stopped the motor and began to sail, bobbing along like a wet sack, the weight of stores and fresh water making progress slow but steady and, most important, in the right direction, east. It was 22 June.

Learning from the experiences with *Silver*, where trim and ballast had been so important, I had designed *Giltspur* very much with these factors in mind, the boat being so much smaller. The compartments in the bottom of the boat, now filled with stores and fresh water, could be filled with seawater as stores were consumed. They were divided by ply walls, like a honeycomb, so that the water would not slop about, causing instability. Space, I knew, was going to be tight, but it was even tighter than I had realized. I had an area only 2 feet wide by 3½ feet long and 18 inches high in which to live, eat and sleep – at least until I did some eating and made more space where stores were now stowed.

I lost sight of Newfoundland during the afternoon. It was very cold and the wind still fresh, but from the northwest, helping me out towards the open ocean. The Newfoundland Banks, the Grand Banks with their mists and cold, lay ahead. Experts in St John's had warned me about icebergs. I had heeded the warning but I did not feel that a boat under 10 feet in length, sailing at about 3 knots, was going to do a repeat of the *Titanic*. Still, I kept a wary eye open for them and there, on that first afternoon, not twenty miles from St John's, were two, right in my path only three or four miles ahead. I sailed between them, the only choice I had under the prevailing wind conditions.

Sickness was an early problem, a result of not having yet found my sealegs coupled with the effect of fumes from my gas cooker and the engine which I used to boost the wind-vane battery charger. There was no escape from it so I simply got on with the business of being sick.

Apart from the sheer misery of it, seasickness presents other problems as well. You have to be careful that these do not cause even more trouble than the actual sickness itself. The first problem is lethargy. It is hard to work and carry out even the simplest tasks, so you actually risk neglecting the boat. Next, you lose strength due to the virtual impossibility of eating or digesting and keeping food down. This, in turn, leads to weakness and cold because there is no fuel to provide body heat. The combination of all these things can reduce a strong man to a useless weakling, incapable of looking after either himself or his boat. In addition, if you are not very strong-willed, you start to experience a feeling of total hopelessness. There is no escape from seasickness unless you manage to get ashore, sail into calm water or are taken aboard a larger and more stable ship – not much chance of that out in the western Atlantic on a dark night.

So I forced myself to eat, attempted simple tasks and eventually, when I was sure it was safe to do so, lay down in a sodden unhappy heap and tried to sleep. I slept fitfully, waking occasionally to be ill, ate some dry food, sipped a little water and kept an eye on the weather. On top of the physical discomforts of seasickness and the psychological depression, there was another problem that I needed to think about and sort out.

I felt miserable, more miserable I reckoned than at almost any previous time of my life. Why? I tried to think it through while I lay there under the small cockpit cover listening to the wind groaning through the rigging and the waves slapping the hull. Then, as I thought about Jill, the children, Ardintigh and home, I realized what it was. I was homesick. Me! Homesick! With my past, it was something I had never experienced before, having never really had a home to be sick about until six years ago. So this was what had new recruits in the barracks at Aldershot blubbering in their beds during those first days in the army. Homesickness. Hurray! I now understood just what home was all about, more than ever. There cannot be many blokes who have been happy to be homesick; in fact I might have even scored a first.

It was a long first night, but I was moving, trying to establish an early routine. Curiously I kept casting my mind back to the voyage with *Silver*. Again it was a matter for thought. Something was missing this time. Then I realized what it was. I did not have to row to go westwards. I was almost missing the business of rowing. All I had to do now was keep the sails filled and *Giltspur* aimed in the right direction. This was a luxury cruise.

Luxury cruise or not, *Giltspur* took quite a bit of work to keep her sailing at about 3 knots, a little under four miles per hour or the pace of a steady walk. It took a good breeze to move her as her short, deep, heavy and somewhat blunt hull was not the best design for fast sailing; there is a limit to the amount of mast and sail that can be carried with safety on such a small boat.

Once moving, she handled well, steering a steady course for hours on end under the guidance of the automatic helm, but once in a while she would stop dead, digging her bow into the sea and slewing to one side or the other without warning or apparent reason. This meant correcting the course, resetting the sails and trimming them.

Another continual problem was the inability of the boat to sail to windward. I found the larger of the jibs was best for windward work, enabling me to sail a little closer than with the other smaller headsails, but whenever the wind went round into the east I felt frustrated, even cheated and angry, as I trimmed the sails in an effort to steal a few miles.

During the first night in fact the wind swung round to the southeast, just what I didn't need, trying to push me towards the Arctic circle. The sea anchor was useless and I was becoming very cold, alternating from a standing position in the back of the small cockpit to a huddled bundle on the floor while the boat pounded and thumped. That was how things were for the first three days as I tried to get my routine under control.

On the fourth day, as I continued to make progress to the northeast, the wind shifted round to the north and freshened to a full Atlantic gale. Christ, it was cold. It was hard to believe that it was late June. It was more like late January in Ardintigh. I took in the sails, deciding finally that just a small jib would suffice, even though waves were breaking right over the boat and soaking everything above and below decks. I pumped the bilges and wrote my logbook. In the front I had written a saying given to me by Donald Davidson.

> If you think you can, you will.
> If you think you can't, you won't.
> The man who wins is the man who thinks he can.

It seemed appropriate now, as I faced my first real storm, surfing down waves that reminded me of the mountains back home. At the foot of that day's entry in the log I wrote simply 'Grim! Grim! Grim!' It was, but my first near-disaster was not far away.

The wind was becoming too much even for the single sail so I decided to take it in. I clambered through the cockpit hatch cover and grabbed the halyard, ready to lower the sail. It clattered down the forestay and I detached the halyard, then the hanks from the stay and finally, with the sail in a wet bundle, the sheet that secured it to the boat. Suddenly a wave like the Niagara Falls hit us, rolling the boat right over onto her side, sweeping the sail from my grasp as I grabbed the side of the cockpit to stop myself falling overboard. As the boat righted I could see the sail in the water about forty yards away, sinking in the white breaking water. One sail gone, five to go. Hell!

The sails stowed, or lost, I went into the space below, pulled the covers over and jammed myself into my crouching corner. The storm was endless, the wind howling even in my small amount of rigging. The vane on the battery charger was howling like a banshee in tune with the wind. Sleep was out of the question, but I went into a comatose doze until dawn when I slid back the hatch and stuck my head out. What a sight! Breaking water as far as the eye could see with a spume of spray scudding across the surface. I remembered a prayer I had seen in a fishing boat in Mallaig.

> The sea is so vast and my boat so small.
> God watch over me.

I think that was how it went, or part of it; it must have been written by someone who had been out here somewhere.

It was time for breakfast, so I managed to light the cooker, boil some water and make a strong mug of tea, open a damp individual packet of cereals, which I ate without milk. They were the sugar-coated sort; perhaps the sugar would do me some good. I felt better after the meal, but as happened on the rowing trip, my feet were playing up. The same old tingling pain was there, a numbness in the toes that suddenly became a screeching agony. I huddled below, removed my boots for the first time since leaving St John's, fumbled with my socks and peeled them off. I unpacked two dry towels and wrapped them round my feet while searching for the lanolin and powder. The feet didn't look too bad, but the toes were puffy and white as if I had spent too long in a hot bath. What a thought! A hot bath. I would give my right foot for one right now.

Amid all this struggle with my feet the boat took a breaking wave over the top, water pouring down my neck, but I dabbed and powdered my feet, finally wrapping them in clean, reasonably dry socks, praising the packers and packing methods of Giltspur. The sealed bags were hard to tear open with wet hands, but the contents were always perfectly dry. Luxury. Remembering the other trip once more, I wrapped my feet in the plastic bags, boots and all, with tape holding the tops of the bags to my legs. It might have looked odd, but I wasn't here for a marine fashion show.

I tidied the cabin area as the wind eased and cooked a meal that became standard. I had tinned and packet foods aboard, the tinned food marked with paint, the labels having been removed. Labels come off in damp conditions and can clog the bilge pump. After a lunch of tinned meat stew, tinned peas and some fruit salad, I checked the outboard which had been in or under water for almost three days. Two pulls on the starter string and the little Suzuki burst into song. So did I. Life was looking up. All I missed was the sun. There had been little or none since leaving Newfoundland and apart from simple bodily warmth, I needed two important pieces of help from the sun: a position fix and the chance to dry clothes, bedding and myself. As it was, the sky remained covered, the fog and mists persisted and the temperature hung around 47° Fahrenheit. What a place. Summer, too.

It was only after two whole rough weeks at sea that I got the winds I really wanted, fresh from the southwest, driving me across the ocean at 3 knots, occasionally, with a surge down a wave front, 4.

For a whole week, the third at sea, the wind stayed in the west, interspersed with patches of misty calm. Calms were almost as bad as storms. They were times of great frustration, the boat rocking in an oily sea, rigging clattering against the mast, progress nil and a feeling of imprisonment on the boat. I would try to catch the breeze, if there was one, with the sails, spending hours shifting ropes and trying to turn the stern towards the whispers of air as they came across the water like the wind over a field of corn.

During the calms I did maintenance work, read, wrote the logbook, took pictures, ate and slept. I also watched for ships, but none came my way. On one calm day the sun broke through and I managed to take a position fix, a rough one, but it made sense against the readings of estimated wind, speed and direction that I had entered in the log. During the storms I wondered how my American rival was faring; the same during the calms when I imagined that he would suddenly appear nearby. He could not be that far away, having started well before me, but having farther to go from his starting point to reach the open ocean. He could still be ahead but, with the weather we had had, I somehow imagined him behind me.

I was, I estimated, about halfway across the Atlantic by the end of the third week, probably helped by my old friend the Gulf Stream, when the easterlies set in. Wind dead on the nose, winds that made me feel that I was being driven back towards Canada. Not just breezes, but good blows right on the nose, like a boxer being outpointed by a heavier opponent.

By the law of averages I should have been able to reach Falmouth in a further three weeks, making the whole crossing in a respectable six weeks. As it is, the law of averages does not exist out on the ocean. As the easterlies blew I tried every trick I knew to make a heading to the east, choosing the tack that took me closest to my destination. At times my efforts seemed futile, but at least I was not going back towards Canada even if I was getting no nearer Europe apart from the help from the prevailing current. This, in turn, running against the wind, was causing lumpy uncomfortable seas.

One amazing fact was that in the entire three weeks I had seen no ships apart from the odd one miles away on the horizon. My efforts at navigation had improved since I rowed the Atlantic but lack of sun had made position fixes unreliable. It was while thinking about the problem that I saw heading towards me a vast container ship looking like a multistorey car park that had been dumped in the sea. I grabbed my VHF radio, selected Channel 16 and called up. She altered course and slowed down, her radio operator having acknowledged my call. They could see me clearly and would stop nearby so that I could move alongside. Did I need anything? I told them that water and my position would be appreciated, as I was down to my last gallon. Although the skies had been overcast for much of the trip there had been very little rain. The ship stopped and I lowered the mainsail, started the outboard and inched towards her.

As the plastic containers of water began to be lowered

towards me, the officer on the bridge shouted down my position. Suddenly the ship began moving again. I was sliding along the side towards the propellers. I shouted up to the bridge, but there was no one in sight. Ineffectively I pushed against the ship's side with my hands, the outboard engine still running and holding me against the ship. The nearest propeller, 4 feet out of the water, was churning remorselessly, threatening to turn the boat into a pulp of matchwood with me wrapped inside. The blades of the wind generator were smashed against the ship's side.

I was shouting and swearing. Suddenly the pressure broke and we were free, swept away from the ship by what must have been a surge from the propeller. The mast, which had become trapped for a moment under the curving stern of the ship, broke free, swinging upwards, the VHF aerial bent at the top like a hairpin. The sail tied to the boom was torn and the boom bent. How the mast was not snapped into two or more pieces, I shall never know, but it survived.

Once away from the ship I gathered myself together, trembling with a combination of rage and physical effort. I didn't even manage to get the name of the ship amid all the confusion. I calmed down and set about getting things ship-shape again. I hoisted the sails and began patching the mainsail with heavy tape. I tried the VHF radio and, to my amazement and delight, found it worked in spite of the condition of the aerial. What was more, as I tuned to Channel 16, I found myself talking to another yacht. A Dutch couple had heard my call to the cargo ship and stayed on listening watch.

We transferred to a working channel, clearing 16 for other traffic. It turned out that the other crew could see the cargo ship so we exchanged bearings to it from our respective boats, worked out our relative positions and steered towards one another. We met. They were Wil and Loes Pennings, from Holland, aboard their British-built yacht *Utopia*. They were on their way from the United States to Falmouth and then onward home to Holland. I had failed to get water from the cargo ship amid all the confusion, so they let me have two gallons. We parted after an enjoyable couple of hours. The wind was light but they were soon over the horizon in their faster yacht. The world felt very empty again.

For ten long days the winds kept in the east, either northeast, due east or southeast. After forty days at sea, having been bumped and banged by the waves for long periods, I began to think of making Ireland my landfall. I was being pushed north of the track for Falmouth, passing the dangers of the Scillies to the south. Another factor that influenced this decision was that I was now picking up Irish radio programmes on my transistor radio – jolly reels and songs, quiz shows that made me laugh, and news of railway strikes in Britain that made me worry about the army teams getting to Ardintigh to do their courses.

Just as when I rowed the Atlantic, I had brought a plastic box of letters with me from friends, to be read on Sundays as a morale booster. The first I opened was from Jill. It started me thinking of home and the kids, and drove me on. Other letters were from friends in London and Scotland, some from the Fun People, others from kids at the local school in Mallaig as part of a project about the trip. One from young Sean O'Donnell, a pupil at the school, really made me think.

'Dear Mr McClean,' he wrote, 'what will you do if a giant octopus comes up out of the sea and kills you, or big black whale or other beastie comes and gobbles you up?'

I could hear his broad but gentle western Scottish brogue coming through the chunky letters on the page. I chuckled as I read it. At that moment there was an enormous bang, nearly lifting me out of the boat. Concorde had passed overhead. At the same instant, perhaps disturbed by the aircraft, a massive whale, its tail higher than the mast, rose alongside, gave a great swoosh of air as it threw a spray of water over the boat, and gently dived, not fifty metres from me. Sean's monster, coming to gobble me up? Half-scared by the bang from Concorde and the closeness of the whale, I started laughing out loud, releasing nervous energy to the sky and sea.

Navigation in such a small boat and in trying weather conditions was a hit-and-miss affair. If there was a good sunsight available at dawn, the sea seemed to be too rough to take a reading on the sextant, my old faithful sextant that had already crossed the Atlantic with me on the rowing trip. I was never unduly worried about my position; in 3000 miles of ocean to be within fifty miles or so of your real position is near enough, but once you begin to close with land you need more accurate information. Noon sights with the sextant seemed to produce better results, but again, they were never good enough to put me in the history books with Christopher Columbus and Vasco da Gama.

My best means of finding out exactly where I was was to stop a merchant ship or call her on the radio and ask her to come over and give me her position, plotted on a satellite navigation system, and put it on my Atlantic chart. There is an amazing comradeship at sea. Never did a ship that I had managed to raise by radio not come and give me the information I wanted. Often, though, the information was just what I could have done without. Whereas my own efforts had put me in one place the work of the merchant shipping navigation officers would push me back about 200 miles or more and I would sit swearing at the damp chart as I plotted the true position. However, towards the end of the voyage, when I was approaching the coast of Ireland and later Cornwall, I was able to pinpoint myself quite accurately, accurately enough to make the right tactical decisions so far as my intended arrival point was concerned.

My thoughts of going to Ireland strengthened as the headwinds continued to pin me out there in the endless ocean. It was only about two hundred miles to the Irish coast but twice that to Falmouth and I had been at sea for forty days, the time I had estimated for the entire crossing. 'PATIENCE', I wrote in the damp logbook, thought hard and long and pressed on. Then came the worst storm of the trip which was to alter thoughts of Ireland to more basic thoughts of survival.

The sky to the northeast was darkening all the time and the barometer began dropping hourly as night approached. I brewed a hot thermos of tea, prepared to take in sail, checked my safety harness, secured loose stores and generally made ready for a tough time. When the storm began in earnest, at the start of my forty-third day at sea, it came in from the north, driving me south. Falmouth, here I come!

At midnight the wind was gusting at what I estimated to be 60 knots and more. It shrieked and howled, bowling the boat on her side as I hunched below in the small space, the hatches pulled shut. I had taken the sails down before the storm broke so the boat was like a cork bobbing about on the heaving wind-flecked sea. It was like a never-ending nightmare, down there, waiting for the boat to break up, be rolled over or simply swamped. None of these things happened, but at least once an hour the end seemed very near and I was pumping every fifteen minutes.

During the storm I caught the fingers of my left hand in the sliding hatch. So firmly fixed were they that I had to use a knife and a screwdriver to lever the hatch open again to free them. The pain was indescribable once the initial numbness wore off. I wrapped them in an emergency field dressing, but it did little to help. They were not broken, but it was obvious that at least one nail was going to come off once the swelling lessened. It was a bad mistake to make at a time when I needed both hands to manage the boat.

Other physical damage was restricted to continually banging my head on the inside of the hatch. If I hit it ten times a day in bad weather, I hit it a hundred times! So often, in fact, that I seemed to have developed a protective pad on the top of my skull.

The storm raged throughout the next day, still pushing me southeast towards Land's End. It was a bad time, my hand causing considerable pain, but the pain and the storm began to ease on the second night. I say 'ease', but the wind only dropped from a severe gale to a full gale and the pain kept pace. Cooking was a problem so I ate foods straight from the tin or packet, supplementing these with vitamin pills. I was short of water again, but the liquid in the tinned fruit and the occasional can of beer helped me through.

The second long night of the storm felt like a lifetime. At dawn I stuck my head out to look around, nearly a fatal mistake. A rogue wave, coming at a different angle from the others, dumped itself on top of the boat as I opened the hatch. Water poured into the boat, rising above the cabin floor, soaking its way into everything, including me. Full of water, the boat was sluggish, not rolling so much as swaying, yawing dangerously. I pumped for my life, but the water took its time to sink to the very lowest part of the boat where the end of the pump lay. It took an hour to get all the water out of the boat, after which I had a meal and hoisted the jib. I was sailing again in the right direction but my transistor radio had been damaged by sea water; my radio programmes were a thing of the past. I missed the radio; it was like having someone else in the boat, someone whom I could turn off when I had had enough of them.

My feet were very bad by now, in spite of efforts to dry them regularly. The weather was moderating all the time so I had another foot-mending session, digging out some dry socks from the locker below the mast, boosting my morale a little once the job was done. The boat was sailing well, the mainsail now hoisted after a repair job to some tears in it, carried out with a surgeon's scalpel and a screwdriver because I couldn't find the sailmaker's needles. I sat in the back of the boat, hatch open and head sticking out in my relaxing and thinking position for fair weather. The sea had moderated with the wind and the sun shone. I was feeling happier than for several days when I saw a ship.

I sailed on, picking up the VHF radio and calling up on Channel 16. They answered, the captain asking if I wanted anything. At first, remembering my last encounter with a ship, I declined their offer, and sailed on past. Then I thought again. What the hell, it couldn't happen twice and I could do with a drop more water, so I turned back and closed with the ship, a cable vessel servicing the transatlantic telephone link. She appeared to be anchored to the seabed by the cable which entered the vessel at one end and dropped back to the bottom at the other while those aboard inspected and serviced the length inside the ship. I started the engine and motored alongside. She was smaller than the other ship and the crew could almost touch the top of my mast from the open deck amidships. As my water container was being filled a bottle of whisky was handed across. I was given my position, offered a bath and generally made to feel welcome. Suddenly the ship began to move while I was still held alongside by the bow rope. I couldn't believe it. Not again!

'Cut the bloody line,' I cried, rushing for my knife.

The boat bumped along the side, the mast crashing against the steel hull. I cut the line and we were swept towards the stern. The radar reflector, the generator vane and the VHF aerial all took a beating as they bumped against the ship's side. I was swearing loudly as I grabbed the engine control to try and back off. The surge of the ship stopped as quickly as it had begun and I was free, busy picking up the bits, but it was a bad moment. Apparently, the ship had some sort of computer controlling her engines to keep her at the right spot on the cable as the currents or tides affected her position.

Once more I was mentally bruised and angry, but, having remembered the other encounter with a ship, I should have left this one alone. I had only myself to blame. I picked up the VHF radio microphone, called the cable ship on Channel 16 and thanked her for her help. At least I had a full stock of water, knew I was within two days' sailing of Land's End, was going in the right direction and was alive and well.

Apart from attempts to contact ships on my limited range VHF set, I had, for the closing days of the voyage, tried to call up radio stations on the west coast of Britain, but I had no proper list of these stations. Using Channel 16, I would call up the Scillies and other coastguard or radio stations that just might have been able to hear me, but with no success.

One plan going through my mind was to put a call through to Harold Wilson, who, I remembered, had a house on the Scillies, and invite him to come and meet me when I arrived at Falmouth. I had always admired him as a person when I had seen him on television so, at that time, it seemed a good idea. He was the only person I had ever heard of from the islands, so what more natural than to ring him up from out in the ocean for a chat. Anyway, he was not there, or the contact with the radio stations in the area did not work, so another hare-brained scheme, one of several that develop when one is alone in the wilds of the ocean, vanished. At least my radio efforts kept my mind on the business in hand even if they were unsuccessful until I was about sixty miles from Cornwall.

That evening I gathered together my kit for my arrival in Britain. It was a good feeling. I checked my emergency landing pack in case I ended up on the dreaded Scillies. I checked the characteristics of lighthouses on the Cornish coast: Bishop Rock, Sevenstones, Wolf Rock and Land's End itself. I also brought the life raft to a more accessible place in the cockpit. I was as ready as I could be for the homecoming from the safety point of view.

Now it was time to think about me. I had not shaved for weeks, had not washed my hair since Canada and probably smelled like a rancid polecat. Next day, my forty-ninth at sea, I would have a real wash, dig out some clean clothes and start behaving like a civilized person again.

That night I thought I could smell land, but as the wind was from the west, blowing across miles of open ocean, this was imagination. I sat sniffing the breeze when I heard and saw an aircraft in the distance – an RAF Nimrod. I grabbed the VHF and called up.

'Nimrod aircraft, this is Tom McClean in yacht *Giltspur*, are you looking for me?'

'Affirmative,' crackled the reply.

'You are four miles to my northwest, repeat, four miles to my northwest.'

The aircraft swung towards me, dropping down towards the sea. A minute later it swooped overhead as the captain, Flight Lieutenant Steve Smith from the RAF's 42 Squadron, asked me what I needed on arrival at Falmouth.

'A large Union Jack, some clean underpants, socks and loo paper,' I replied.

He laughed, congratulated me, gave me an exact position and a course to steer for a passage south of the Scillies and was on his way eastwards. I felt great. That night I called up Land's End and talked to Jill direct after the radio operators, the coastguards at Falmouth and others, had broken every rule in the radio operators' book to patch me through to her at the hotel in Falmouth where she was staying.

Magic. We had a long chat and she told me that the Fun People were there as well as many journalists. She sounded as if she was sitting on deck, so good was the link. We agreed to talk again later, once a more legal link could be tied together.

I then had the washing session, using at least a gallon of fresh water, and felt great when it was done. Away to the northeast I could see the loom of the Bishop Rock lighthouse. I was safe from the Scillies, making a good course for home.

No sleep that night: there was a mass of fishing boats about and I was not going to risk a collision now.

Next morning, at dawn, I could make out the low outline of the Cornish coast to the north of Land's End. The tides were strong now, sweeping me towards the Lizard headland for six hours and then setting against me for six more. There were whirlpools and breaking waves at times, occasionally turning the boat right around. In Mounts Bay, to the west of the Lizard, I was met by the Fun People who had chartered a fast boat and brought out my extra stores, the vast flag, the spare clothing and the loo paper. What luxury!

I rounded the Lizard that evening and headed for Falmouth as darkness fell. I had told Jill that I would stay out until next morning, so had to find a place to spend the night. I looked at the chart and saw the entrance to the Helford river. South of the river mouth was a village called Gillan, sheltered from the west. I made for that, dropped anchor among other boats and sat in the cockpit watching the lights twinkling on the shore nearby. I called Jill again and told her where I was, but asked her not to tell anyone until first thing next day. Then I made a meal, poured a good strong drink and slept like a child.

I was up with the dawn, a fine bright day. Only boats and a few rocks surrounded me as I brewed some coffee. My peace was short-lived. Two launches appeared from the direction of Falmouth, packed with rival television crews who took it in turn to film me as I set sail. There was no sign of Jill; she had gone aboard the press boat which, in spite of my instructions, was steaming out towards the Lizard, missing Gillan Creek by several miles. They eventually turned back and as I sailed the final miles to the entrance to Falmouth harbour Jill was alongside. The cliffs were lined by crowds, spectator craft came to meet me, a yacht almost cut me in two inside the harbour, but I had made it.

15 Aftermath

The welcome ashore at Falmouth was tremendous. Half Cornwall seemed to be on the pier at the Greenbank Hotel. The press were there in force asking hundreds of questions, most just short of stupid. I was asked about my physical condition and replied by challenging the questioner to a hundred press-ups or a handstand, or both. One thing I really wanted was a hot bath, but even in the bathroom in my suite in the hotel there was no escaping the photographers. Someone produced a rubber boat and the photographers took pictures of me sitting in the bath holding it – Tom McClean and his bathtub boat.

I asked about Bill Dunlop. Nothing had been heard of him for almost two weeks, the time when I was battling against one of the big Atlantic storms. I wished him no harm but have to admit that the news that he had abandoned his voyage would have made me a happy man. I wanted the record, which at that time I held, for the crossing in the smallest boat, so all I could do was wait and see.

Alec Beilby, from the *Sunday Express*, took my logbook and the tape recordings I had made on the voyage and disappeared to start getting my story together. It was Thursday and Sir John Junor had decided to run the story three days later. It was needed in London by midday on Friday. There was work to be done and a long night ahead if we were to meet the deadline.

Jill looked wonderful in spite of all the worries that she had faced during the closing days of the journey and we had a celebration lunch with the people from Giltspur as well as the friends from Scotland and Yorkshire who had come down to meet me. After that I set to work with Alec who was confident we could manage to produce a full-page feature on the first half of the voyage for the coming Sunday and the second half a week later. Like everything else in the boat, my logbook was a sodden mass, but it held together after being carefully dried out in an oven in the hotel kitchen. The films I had shot aboard *Giltspur* were collected and sent to London for rapid processing. The boat was taken away by friends to a local boatyard where it was unloaded and given a good cleaning below decks. Many items still in the airtight bags that the Giltspur company had heat-sealed before I sailed were as good as the day they were packed.

Next morning it was champagne for breakfast, provided by some of the Fun People, before finishing the story which Alec then filed to the paper in London, a telephone call that took almost two hours. It took so long, in fact, that he and the reporter taking it down on a typewriter at the other end of the line had to stop halfway through so that they could each have a rest and a pint of beer, Alec in Cornwall and the copy-taker in a Fleet Street pub. Then, after a final dinner with the many friends who were still celebrating, it was almost time to set off to stay with friends nearby in Cornwall, Den and Helen Collam, who have always made me very welcome. But not before one more task, carried out at the request of the local coastguards who had been such a help with radio links during the final days of the trip to Falmouth.

A lone sailor was in port waiting to set sail into the ocean in a boat that, in my opinion, would probably not have crossed the Carrick Roads, off Falmouth. He had painted a cross on the cabin roof and seemed to have a death wish. Though they could not stop him from sailing, the coastguards had tried, unsuccessfully, to persuade him not to go. I met him and, quite frankly, was not impressed with his physical ability, his mental approach or his boat. We had a long chat and, as far as I know, he decided against the idea of sailing.

All this while my thoughts were still on the ocean wondering about Bill Dunlop. Where was he? Was he still sailing or had he been picked up by a cargo ship after a storm? Even the fantastic press coverage that my arrival had received, with cartoons in the national morning papers, couldn't take my mind off it. I wanted to keep my record but not at the expense of another man's life. Later, when I met Bill at the London Boat Show, we compared notes and his thoughts, while still battling his way across the ocean, had been very similar about me.

After a short stop in Cornwall, which included a visit to see Chay and Maureen Blyth, we headed for Surrey to spend some time with Phil Rhodes in his beautiful home near Haslemere. There was a party for Trevor Moore to celebrate his fortieth birthday and the house was a good base for visits to London to talk to agents. We also went to Southampton, to the Giltspur main depot where my boat had been taken. I was to sail her again among the mighty tall ships at the end of their race from Spain.

I found an agent who promised to arrange a number of talks for me to give about the voyage and then set off with Jill to her family and the children in Yorkshire. Wanda gave us a surprise welcome home party with balloons and streamers. She had fastened all the press cuttings and a chart of the North Atlantic to the wall. All the family had a great time and there was even a cake which had been made in the shape of *Giltspur*. James seemed to realize that something fairly important had happened, but was still too young to understand what I had done. That could wait until he was older. Then we heard that Bill Dunlop had been sighted off Land's End by RAF Nimrods. He was on his way in the smallest boat and arrived a couple of days later to a welcome, I was told, as exciting and enthusiastic as the one I had received. The Cornish people really are wonderful when it comes to welcoming seafarers. Ah, well, I thought, well done him. But in my heart there was a deep niggle of disappointment. A plan was already forming, but there was a great deal to be sorted out back at Ardintigh where the centre had been run by Gerry Holland, a recently retired army major, for the past three months.

We drove north to Scotland where great surprise celebrations lay in store. Any Doubting Thomases at Mallaig and elsewhere were silent or among the first to offer their congratulations. After a few days at Ardintigh getting back into the routine, Jill and I were enticed back to the town where the whole population lay in wait at the Marine Hotel for a surprise party that went on well into the night. Now I was really one of them, the west-coast Highland people – one of the family, and it felt very good.

During the early winter I went to London to discuss plans for the Boat Show stand at Earl's Court where the presenters, the *Daily Express*, wanted to put my boat alongside Bill Dunlop's as a special Atlantic sailors feature. At last I would meet my rival.

Plans were already in hand for my next scheme. Bill's boat was 8 inches shorter than mine and that had earned him the record. Answer? Saw 9 inches off the bow and stern of *Giltspur*, making her 1 inch shorter than *Wind's Will*, and do the voyage again. I had to get the record back for Britain, but it had to be a secret in case some other sailor, or even Bill himself, had it in mind to do something similar. Anyway, no alterations could be made until the London Boat Show was over because they wanted the boat as she had been for the voyage.

Back north once more for a happy Christmas and New Year at home with the family. We spent New Year's Eve across the creek at Cameron's house with some of the Fun People. It was almost a bad start to the year when a violent storm blew up in the middle of the night, breaking the big launch, *Gypsy Rover*, from her mooring. It was like earlier days when boats had taken off by themselves. She was well down the loch by the time we noticed she was missing so I shot off into the storm in the rescue boat with only the small Seagull outboard for power. I caught *Gypsy Rover* before she hit the rocks where, certainly, she would have been a total wreck. It was a sharp reminder that up on the loch one can never completely forget that it is the weather that rules one's life.

Then it was time to go to London for the Boat Show. The New Year sales were on and Jill had a gleam in her eye. Our stand at the show was impressive, the two little boats being set on a long platform against a painted backdrop of the ocean. I had never realized just how tiring it is to man a stand at an exhibition, although I had done the same thing in 1970 after the rowing trip across the Atlantic. Was I really beginning to feel older?

The crowds began coming even before the show was officially opened by the First Sea Lord, Admiral Sir John Fieldhouse, who, during his tour of the show after the opening ceremony, spent a long time talking to Jill and me. He seemed fascinated and amazed by the boat. If he thought I was slightly mad he never showed it. What none of us knew was that the very next day he was to leave Britain with the Prime Minister for Mrs Thatcher's surprise visit to the Falkland Islands. When I heard the news of the visit I wondered what the Admiral's thoughts had been as he called at the Falklands' display a few yards down the aisle from mine.

We met old and new friends every day from morning until mid-evening and then met more friends after the show closed. Faces would appear at the stand from every part of Britain. The problem was, I found, putting a name to some of them. One often connects a face to a place and Earl's Court was a strange place from that point of view. Often I had to apologize to someone whom I had known well in Saudi Arabia, Scotland, the orphanage or elsewhere simply because I was caught off guard by their sudden appearance amid the hundreds of strange faces that passed every hour.

Finally the show ended, we packed the stand and the Giltspur company sent a truck to take the boat back to Ardintigh. Bill and his wife Pam said a friendly farewell to us; he was off to the United States to start a cruise in *Wind's Will* of both sides of the country. I had announced my next plan, to take back the record, while at the Boat Show and he wished me the best of luck and bon voyage in the friendliest possible way. He was as great a man as I had always suspected. He promised, one day, to come and stay at Ardintigh and offered us the same hospitality at his home at Mechanic Falls, Maine. Meanwhile we both have travelling to do.

16 Final Thoughts and New Plans

Back in Scotland after the Boat Show, it was time to start preparing for the next trip, my attempt to retrieve the transatlantic record for the crossing in the smallest boat for Britain. I had talked to Giltspur about sponsoring this second voyage but they would not commit themselves. Certainly they benefited from having their name on the side of the boat at the Boat Show and they were good enough to provide a lorry and a driver to take the boat back to Mallaig where Johnston Brothers, the ship's chandlers, were to look after her until I arrived home. Back in Mallaig, I received the letter that I had been half expecting from the Giltspur group. They had decided not to continue their support for the next voyage. I had to find a new sponsor.

Time was getting tight if I was to shorten the boat enough to enable me to claim a new record, not from Bill Dunlop, but now from the young American, Wayne Dickinson, who, after 146 days at sea, had reached the coast of western Ireland in his boat *God's Tear*, a mere 8 feet 11 inches long.

Wayne Dickinson's crossing impressed me. He had proved yet again that if the boat is properly built it will survive the crossing. His crossing had been made during one of the worst winters that the Mallaig fishermen could remember, but, unlike me, he had drifted most of the way which is why he took so long. He was apparently seeking evidence as to whether or not God existed. Everyone to his own choice. He survived and when last heard of was setting up a home on the Irish coast near where he had landed. He was lucky and he probably found the answers he was seeking. But I, meanwhile, had to find a sponsor.

Richard Butler of Extel, who had helped on the first voyage, was sending out letters to companies, but by 10 February, when the rays of the winter sun touched the roof of the camp at Ardintigh for the first time after the long dark winter days, we had no offers of help to finance the project.

Rod Wood came up from Dalkeith and we towed the boat from Mallaig to Ardintigh. To get some publicity for my voyage, and thereby perhaps attract a sponsor, I decided to make a bit of a fuss of the shortening of the boat. We could have done it with a hand saw, working quietly up the loch, but I invited the BBC Television and the press to the occasion and, having drawn a line round the stern section of the boat, I took a chain saw and lopped off 11 inches. I hit the headlines right across the country and even managed to earn a full page in the London *Standard*. Surely someone who would be prepared to help would read that.

Once the press had left, the real work began. By removing the stern, I had given myself a golden opportunity to redesign and refit the interior through the gaping hole where the stern section had been. I altered the honeycomb lockers under the floor and built a number of small lockers and cupboards on either side for storing everyday things. Storage had been a problem on the first voyage and with a smaller boat it was going to be a greater problem unless I made careful adjustments to the space below deck.

The boat was turning into a space capsule. Everything had to have its proper place where it would be immediately to hand, everything from food to distress flares, survival kit and toiletries – loo paper, toothbrush and soap. I started in the bow, and gradually worked my way out of the back of the boat, giving the accommodation a coat of paint as I went. Finally, across the stern I built a new bulkhead to which I screwed and glued the new stern section. This made the new section very strong, probably stronger than before.

One problem was to redesign the rudder, which was

becoming shorter and shorter. I extended it to twice its former length by adding an extra piece. During subsequent trials it worked, making the boat very manoeuvrable while acting as an extension of the keel when locked in the fore and aft position.

Out on the green at Ardintigh working on the boat, I found the old urge to start sailing again come back with a vengeance. I could not wait to ship the boat to Canada and get cracking. It was cold out on the green, rain, sleet and snow coming down on us in sheets as we worked, but we finished the job.

Rod Wood came for Easter and helped fit the rudder and the other bits and pieces that hung on the stern – the outboard engine mounting, the wind generator and the foot holds for climbing down the stern if necessary.

I still had no major sponsor. I had a few little flickers of interest from one or two people, but nothing positive. I tried the *Mary Rose* Trust again, but received no immediate response. The *Sunday Express* indicated that they would buy the exclusive story again and I awaited their contract. If they confirmed their offer and if an idea for taking 5000 first-day covers to sell when I got back materialized, then I could afford to ship the boat to Canada and fly over at the end of May. After the building, getting the boat to Canada is the most expensive part of the game. After that it is all down hill so far as money is concerned. The wind is free and there are no shops, bank managers or other financial hazards in mid-Atlantic.

Various people had been suggesting that this challenge of crossing the Atlantic, in which size, not speed, was the crucial factor, was turning into a version of the famous Atlantic Blue Riband for which the great ocean liners used to compete. Blue Riband became my name for the trip from then on.

I worked on, fitting new equipment which had been donated by people whom I had met at the Boat Show. A satellite navigator arrived from Walkers as well as two VHF radios from another company. My CB radio had proved useless last time so I decided to replace it with more practical equipment that would give me a better chance of talking to the outside world. I was using the same mast and sails but altered some of the deck fittings. By mid-April, apart from stores and ballasting, I was ready to go. Some Officer Training Corps cadets came to the camp for the Easter period and, loth to miss an opportunity, I got them to help carry the boat from the green outside the huts to the sea. The boat weighed over half a ton unladen and we had quite a struggle, but she floated exactly right. I was a happy man, raring to get back out into the ocean. I was also looking forward to seeing my Canadian friends in St John's again and sent off a few letters warning them of my new plan. Replies came thick and fast.

Provisionally I had planned to ship the boat out from Liverpool by Dart containers but on the off-chance I put a call through to Cunard in Liverpool and managed to find someone who, it appeared, was responsible for the freight side of their operations. As I write this I wait to hear what they can offer, but my idea is for them to ship it over free and, in exchange, I will do a cruise on the *QE II* or one of their other liners, with the boat aboard in one of the assembly areas, and give lectures to the passengers.

People were still asking why I wanted to go again. My answer is the same as last time. It is another adventure, another challenge. I enjoy myself out there on the ocean, particularly if I'm winning something for Britain. Other people raise their eyebrows at my apparent irresponsibility in leaving my wife and two small kids at home while I go out and chance my luck. During an evening at the pub in Mallaig, the disc jockey, the leader of a local group, played a request for me, announcing it as a song for Tom McClean who crossed the Atlantic in a bottletop and was about to try again. The word 'try' was wrong; he should have said that I was about to do it again. His jibe about the bottletop did not bother me. I had just bought Jill a home at Morar, a six-bedroom house with views right across the Sound of Sleat all the way to Skye and the Small Islands.

I have other adventures in my mind. Rockall, that lonely rock that lies away out in the Atlantic to the west of the Hebrides, might need my help. Every year or two the Royal Navy land men there and hoist the Union Jack, claiming the rock for Britain. My scheme is to ask the Navy to land me there with a Portakabin which I would bolt and concrete to the rock. I would live there for a month or two each year, opening a post office and establishing an address. Then it really would be part of the UK should anyone have any doubts.

Just think of it, think of the address.

Tom McClean
The Post Office
Rockall
Eastern Atlantic
UK

No, I must go again out into the ocean. The urge for adventure is still in me and while it is there I will keep on looking for things that provide a challenge. As I have said, I calculate every risk I take. I plan carefully, stay prepared to meet difficulty and try to anticipate trouble before it happens. That is the way I have been brought up right from the first battles all those years ago in the orphanage, through the training in the Parachute Regiment and on into the Special Air Service. Those days, in my opinion, were the grounding for what I have done since, be it hacking my home out of the Scottish hills, rowing the ocean or sailing it. It might not be everyone's idea of a life; some people seem to enjoy taking the same train every day to sit at the same desk and see the same faces. I could no more face that than they could survive a winter at Ardintigh or cross the ocean alone in a very small boat.

All I hope is that my exploits as I have described them here will help to show that there are many ways of living one's life, even in these modern times, where the basic ingredients for survival are the senses given us, our own strength and a strong desire to overcome anything that nature can throw at us.

Index

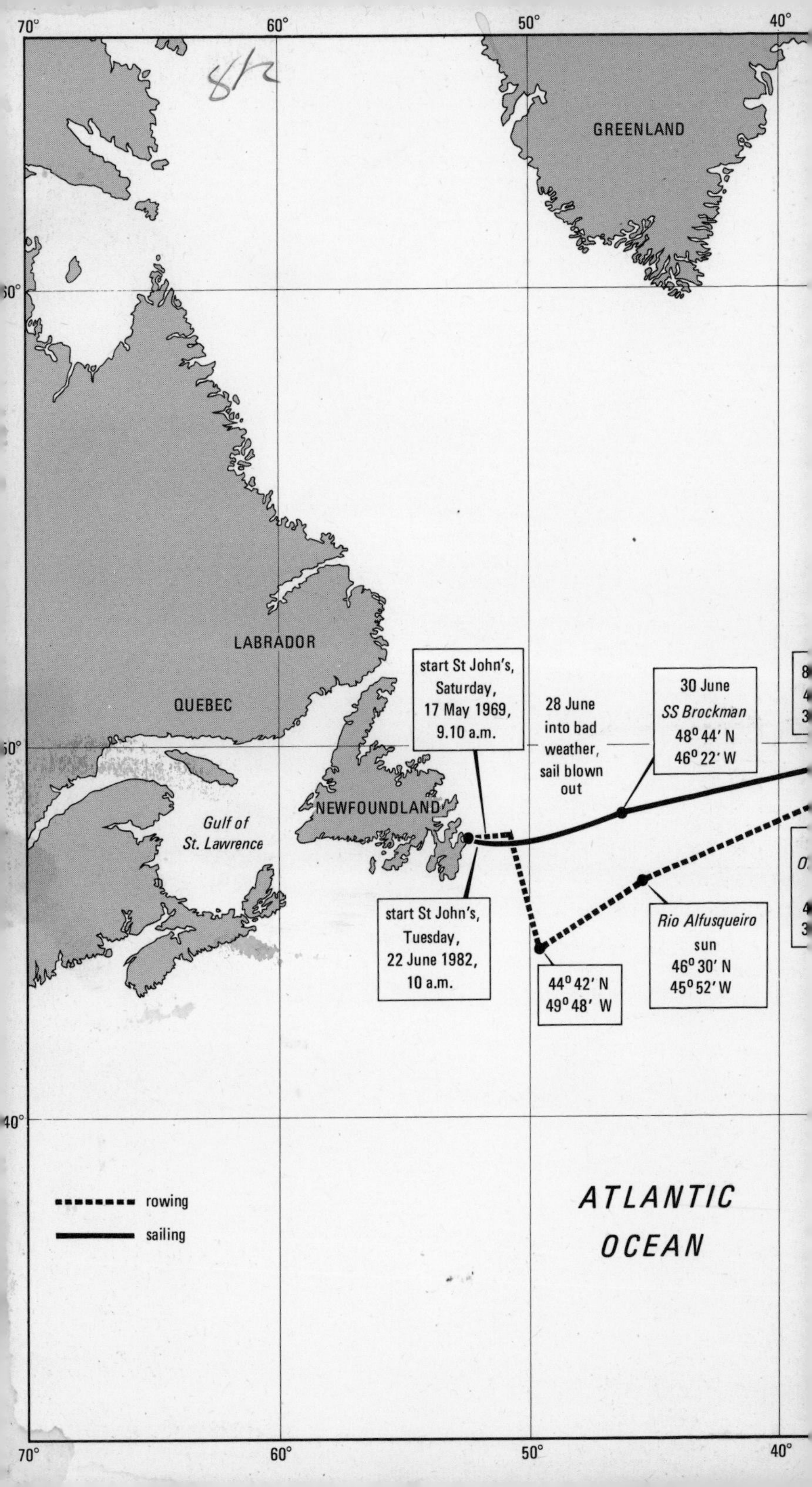
70°
60°
50°
40°
GREENLAND
LABRADOR
QUEBEC
NEWFOUNDLAND
Gulf of
St. Lawrence
start St John's,
Saturday,
17 May 1969,
9.10 a.m.
28 June
into bad
weather,
sail blown
out
30 June
SS Brockman
48° 44′ N
46° 22′ W
start St John's,
Tuesday,
22 June 1982,
10 a.m.
44° 42′ N
49° 48′ W
Rio Alfusqueiro
sun
46° 30′ N
45° 52′ W
rowing
sailing
ATLANTIC
OCEAN
40°